Alfred Tennyson

Lyrical Poems

Alfred Tennyson

Lyrical Poems

ISBN/EAN: 9783744779586

Printed in Europe, USA, Canada, Australia, Japan

Cover: Foto ©Thomas Meinert / pixelio.de

More available books at **www.hansebooks.com**

LYRICAL POEMS

BY

ALFRED

LORD TENNYSON

SELECTED AND ANNOTATED

BY

FRANCIS T. PALGRAVE

London
MACMILLAN AND CO.
1885

TO
EMILY
LADY TENNYSON

My dear Lady Tennyson:

Many years ago, when Hallam and Lionel were hardly older than "golden-hair'd Ally" himself, it was my happy fortune to be allowed the honour of dedicating the "Golden Treasury" to the Poet Laureate. During a walk near the Land's End, which is still fresh in my memory, I had placed the scheme of the book before him: —but, on learning that my plan included the best lyrics by writers then alive, and only the best, he at once barred any pieces by him from insertion within an anthology bearing a title which, in itself, seemed to claim the honours of excellence for the contents. And so very large a portion of admissible contemporary song was banished by this decree, that limitation to the poetry of those no longer alive became inevitable.

That deficiency is, however, now supplied, to the best of my power, in the Treasury, not less worthy the title Golden, with the formation of which I have been entrusted. You have allowed me, in this Dedication, to grace it with a name honoured, wherever Lord Tennyson's is known, as that of the one—

Dear, near, and true

to him from youth to age,—the counsellor to whom he has never looked in vain for aid and comfort,—the Wife whose perfect love has blessed him through these many years with large and faithful sympathy.—And it is my hope that you will not find your favour ill-bestowed, although, (through the strict limits of space imposed), you will necessarily miss here some choice flowers from that Vergilian Garden which your own Poet has added to the realm,— already so wealthy and so wide,—of England's Helicon.

It is not in the crowd, not in the study, that Poetry,—Lyrical Poetry in especial, as the deepest and nearest to the heart,—can most efficiently perform her natural " happy-making" function :—can, as the Laureate's great Predecessor said, " add sunshine to daylight," lift us out of ourselves, and even give a foreglimpse of that other world, without faith in which, this fair earth itself is but a " land of the shadow of death, and where the light is as darkness." —*" A grace," as the finest and wisest of our humourists once remarked, is wanted " before Poetry ";—and this, I think, may best be found where her still, sweet voice is heard amidst the beauty of Nature, alone, or " when hearts are of each other sure," and sea or torrent, forest or mountain-side, supply a landscape worthy the presence of the Muses and their divine Leader. It is for such fit audience that I have endeavoured in this, as in three or four other little books, to provide companionship; these, methinks, are the true " editions of luxury":—with me, not with my material, is the fault, if a selection from the best work of the world's greatest living Poet does not, amply and delightfully, fulfil its proper function.*

F. T. PALGRAVE

Jan. 1885

*— VOS O LAURI CARPAM ET TE PROXIMA MYRTE,
SIC POSITAE QUONIAM SUAVIS MISCETIS ODORES.*

CONTENTS

	PAGE
TO THE QUEEN	1
A DREAM OF FAIR WOMEN	3
THE PALACE OF ART	11
LOCKSLEY HALL	20
THE MAY QUEEN	31
IN THE CHILDREN'S HOSPITAL	38
THE GRANDMOTHER	42
RIZPAH	48
THE VISION OF SIN	54
THE TWO VOICES	60
WAGES	74
THE SAILOR BOY	75
THE VOYAGE	76
THE DAY-DREAM	79
THE SEA-FAIRIES	88
THE LOTOS-EATERS	89
THE VOYAGE OF MAELDUNE	94
THE DYING SWAN	101
THE BROOK	103
THE DAISY	105
TO THE REV. F. D. MAURICE	108
NORTHERN FARMER (Old Style)	110
NORTHERN FARMER (New Style)	114
THE NORTHERN COBBLER	118

	PAGE
Will Waterproof's Lyrical Monologue	124
The Poet's Song	131
To ——	132
Alcaics	133
The Lady of Shalott	134
Sir Launcelot and Queen Guinevere	138
Sir Galahad	140
St. Agnes' Eve	142
A Farewell	143
'Come not when I am Dead'	144
'Hapless Doom of Woman'	144
'Ask me no more'	144
'Sweet and Low'	145
'What does Little Birdie say'	145
'O let the Solid Ground'	146
'Birds in the High Hall-Garden'	146
'Go not, Happy Day'	147
'Rivulet crossing my Ground'	148
'Come into the Garden, Maud'	149
'I have led her Home'	151
'O that 'twere Possible'	154
'Tears, Idle Tears'	157
'Late, late, so late'	157
'Turn, Fortune, turn thy Wheel'	158
'In Love, if Love be Love'	158
'Sweet is true Love'	159
Mariana	159
Mariana in the South	161
The Sisters	164
The Lord of Burleigh	165
Lady Clara Vere de Vere	168
The Beggar Maid	170
The Talking Oak	170

	PAGE
MILKMAID'S SONG	179
THE MILLER'S DAUGHTER	179
THE LETTERS	186
TO J. S.	187
'YOU ASK ME, WHY, THO' ILL AT EASE'	190
'OF OLD SAT FREEDOM ON THE HEIGHTS'	190
'LOVE THOU THY LAND'	191
THE REVENGE	194
ODE ON THE DEATH OF THE DUKE OF WELLINGTON	200
THE CHARGE OF THE LIGHT BRIGADE	207
THE DEFENCE OF LUCKNOW	209
'BREAK, BREAK, BREAK'	214
IN THE VALLEY OF CAUTERETZ	215
'THIS TRUTH CAME BORNE WITH BIER AND PALL'	215
'I HEAR THE NOISE ABOUT THY KEEL'	219
'CALM IS THE MORN WITHOUT A SOUND'	219
'TEARS OF THE WIDOWER, WHEN HE SEES'	220
'IF ONE SHOULD BRING ME THIS REPORT'	221
''TIS WELL; 'TIS SOMETHING; WE MAY STAND'	221
'THE DANUBE TO THE SEVERN GAVE'	222
'WITH WEARY STEPS I LOITER ON'	222
'PEACE; COME AWAY: THE SONG OF WOE'	223
'IN THOSE SAD WORDS I TOOK FAREWELL'	223
'AS SOMETIMES IN A DEAD MAN'S FACE'	224
'HE TASTED LOVE WITH HALF HIS MIND'	224
'WHEN ROSY PLUMELETS TUFT THE LARCH'	225
'NOW FADES THE LAST LONG STREAK OF SNOW'	225
'IS IT, THEN, REGRET FOR BURIED TIME'	226
'DOORS, WHERE MY HEART WAS USED TO BEAT'	226
'THERE ROLLS THE DEEP WHERE GREW THE TREE'	227

	PAGE
'Old Yew, which graspest at the Stones'	227
'One writes, that "Other Friends remain"'	228
'The Lesser Griefs that may be said'	229
'I envy not in any Moods'	230
'The Time draws near the Birth of Christ'	230
'When Lazarus left his Charnel-Cave'	231
'Her Eyes are Homes of Silent Prayer'	231
'O thou that after Toil and Storm'	232
'Tho' Truths in Manhood darkly join'	232
'Could we forget the Widow'd Hour'	233
'Be near me when my Light is Low'	234
'Do we indeed desire the Dead'	234
'Oh yet we trust that somehow Good'	235
'He past; a Soul of Nobler Tone'	235
'Dost thou look back on what hath been'	236
'I dream'd there would be Spring no more'	237
'Sweet after Showers, Ambrosial Air'	237
'How pure at Heart and sound in Head'	238
'My Love has talk'd with Rocks and Trees'	238
'Risest thou thus, Dim Dawn, again'	239
'I climb the Hill: from End to End'	240
'Unwatch'd, the Garden Bough shall sway'	241
'Again at Christmas did we weave'	241
'Ring out, Wild Bells, to the Wild Sky'	242
'O Living Will that shalt endure'	243
Notes	245
Index of First Lines	267

TO THE QUEEN

Revered, beloved—O you that hold
   A nobler office upon earth
     Than arms, or power of brain, or birth
Could give the warrior kings of old,

Victoria,—since your Royal grace
   To one of less desert allows
     This laurel greener from the brows
Of him that utter'd nothing base;

And should your greatness, and the care
   That yokes with empire, yield you time
     To make demand of modern rhyme
If aught of ancient worth be there;

Then—while a sweeter music wakes,
   And thro' wild March the throstle calls,
     Where all about your palace-walls
The sun-lit almond-blossom shakes—

Take, Madam, this poor book of song;
   For tho' the faults were thick as dust
     In vacant chambers, I could trust
Your kindness.   May you rule us long,

And leave us rulers of your blood
  As noble till the latest day!
  May children of your children say,
'She wrought her people lasting good;

'Her court was pure; her life serene;
  God gave her peace; her land reposed;
  A thousand claims to reverence closed
In her as Mother, Wife, and Queen;

'And statesmen at her council met
  Who knew the seasons when to take
  Occasion by the hand, and make
The bounds of freedom wider yet

'By shaping some august decree,
  Which kept her throne unshaken still,
  Broad-based upon her people's will,
And compass'd by the inviolate sea.'

March 1851

I

A DREAM OF FAIR WOMEN

I read, before my eyelids dropt their shade,
  '*The Legend of Good Women,*' long ago
Sung by the morning star of song, who made
  His music heard below;

Dan Chaucer, the first warbler, whose sweet breath
  Preluded those melodious bursts that fill
The spacious times of great Elizabeth
  With sounds that echo still.

And, for a while, the knowledge of his art
  Held me above the subject, as strong gales
Hold swollen clouds from raining, tho' my heart,
  Brimful of those wild tales,

Charged both mine eyes with tears. In every land
  I saw, wherever light illumineth,
Beauty and anguish walking hand in hand
  The downward slope to death.

Those far-renowned brides of ancient song
  Peopled the hollow dark, like burning stars,
And I heard sounds of insult, shame, and wrong,
  And trumpets blown for wars;

And clattering flints batter'd with clanging hoofs;
  And I saw crowds in column'd sanctuaries;
And forms that pass'd at windows and on roofs
  Of marble palaces;

Corpses across the threshold; heroes tall
   Dislodging pinnacle and parapet
Upon the tortoise creeping to the wall;
   Lances in ambush set;

And high shrine-doors burst thro' with heated blasts
   That run before the fluttering tongues of fire;
White surf wind-scatter'd over sails and masts,
   And ever climbing higher;

Squadrons and squares of men in brazen plates,
   Scaffolds, still sheets of water, divers woes,
Ranges of glimmering vaults with iron grates,
   And hush'd seraglios.

So shape chased shape as swift as, when to land
   Bluster the winds and tides the self-same way,
Crisp foam-flakes scud along the level sand,
   Torn from the fringe of spray.

I started once, or seem'd to start in pain,
   Resolved on noble things, and strove to speak,
As when a great thought strikes along the brain,
   And flushes all the cheek.

And once my arm was lifted to hew down
   A cavalier from off his saddle-bow,
That bore a lady from a leaguer'd town;
   And then, I know not how,

All those sharp fancies, by down-lapsing thought
   Stream'd onward, lost their edges, and did creep
Roll'd on each other, rounded, smooth'd, and brought
   Into the gulfs of sleep.

At last methought that I had wander'd far
   In an old wood: fresh-wash'd in coolest dew
The maiden splendours of the morning star
   Shook in the stedfast blue.

Enormous elm-tree-boles did stoop and lean
   Upon the dusky brushwood underneath
Their broad curved branches, fledged with clearest green,
   New from its silken sheath.

The dim red morn had died, her journey done,
    And with dead lips smiled at the twilight plain,
Half-fall'n across the threshold of the sun,
    Never to rise again.

There was no motion in the dumb dead air,
    Not any song of bird or sound of rill;
Gross darkness of the inner sepulchre
    Is not so deadly still

As that wide forest. Growths of jasmine turn'd
    Their humid arms festooning tree to tree,
And at the root thro' lush green grasses burn'd
    The red anemone.

I knew the flowers, I knew the leaves, I knew
    The tearful glimmer of the languid dawn
On those long, rank, dark wood-walks drench'd in dew,
    Leading from lawn to lawn.

The smell of violets, hidden in the green,
    Pour'd back into my empty soul and frame
The times when I remember to have been
    Joyful and free from blame.

And from within me a clear under-tone
    Thrill'd thro' mine ears in that unblissful clime,
'Pass freely thro': the wood is all thine own,
    Until the end of time.'

At length I saw a lady within call,
    Stiller than chisell'd marble, standing there;
A daughter of the gods, divinely tall,
    And most divinely fair.

Her loveliness with shame and with surprise
    Froze my swift speech: she turning on my face
The star-like sorrows of immortal eyes,
    Spoke slowly in her place.

'I had great beauty: ask thou not my name:
    No one can be more wise than destiny.
Many drew swords and died. Where'er I came
    I brought calamity.'

'No marvel, sovereign lady: in fair field
    Myself for such a face had boldly died,'
I answer'd free; and turning I appeal'd
    To one that stood beside.

But she, with sick and scornful looks averse,
    To her full height her stately stature draws;
'My youth,' she said, 'was blasted with a curse:
    This woman was the cause.

'I was cut off from hope in that sad place,
    Which men call'd Aulis in those iron years
My father held his hand upon his face;
    I, blinded with my tears,

'Still strove to speak: my voice was thick with sighs
    As in a dream. Dimly I could descry
The stern black-bearded kings with wolfish eyes,
    Waiting to see me die.

'The high masts flicker'd as they lay afloat;
    The crowds, the temples, waver'd, and the shore;
The bright death quiver'd at the victim's throat;
    Touch'd; and I knew no more.'

Whereto the other with a downward brow:
    'I would the white cold heavy-plunging foam,
Whirl'd by the wind, had roll'd me deep below,
    Then when I left my home.'

Her slow full words sank thro' the silence drear,
    As thunder-drops fall on a sleeping sea:
Sudden I heard a voice that cried, 'Come here,
    That I may look on thee.'

I turning saw, throned on a flowery rise,
    One sitting on a crimson scarf unroll'd;
A queen, with swarthy cheeks and bold black eyes,
    Brow-bound with burning gold.

She, flashing forth a haughty smile, began:
    'I govern'd men by change, and so I sway'd
All moods. 'Tis long since I have seen a man.
    Once, like the moon, I made

A Dream of Fair Women

'The ever-shifting currents of the blood
  According to my humour ebb and flow.
I have no men to govern in this wood:
  That makes my only woe

'Nay—yet it chafes me that I could not bend
  One will; nor tame and tutor with mine eye
That dull cold-blooded Cæsar. Prythee, friend,
  Where is Mark Antony?

'The man, my lover, with whom I rode sublime
  On Fortune's neck: we sat as God by God:
The Nilus would have risen before his time
  And flooded at our nod.

'We drank the Libyan Sun to sleep, and lit
  Lamps which out-burn'd Canopus. O my life
In Egypt! O the dalliance and the wit,
  The flattery and the strife,

'And the wild kiss, when fresh from war's alarms,
  My Hercules, my Roman Antony,
My mailed Bacchus leapt into my arms,
  Contented there to die!

'And there he died: and when I heard my name
  Sigh'd forth with life I would not brook my fear
Of the other: with a worm I balk'd his fame.
  What else was left? look here!'

(With that she tore her robe apart, and half
  The polish'd argent of her breast to sight
Laid bare. Thereto she pointed with a laugh,
  Showing the aspick's bite.)

'I died a Queen. The Roman soldier found
  Me lying dead, my crown about my brows,
A name for ever!—lying robed and crown'd,
  Worthy a Roman spouse.'

Her warbling voice, a lyre of widest range
  Struck by all passion, did fall down and glance
From tone to tone, and glided thro' all change
  Of liveliest utterance.

When she made pause I knew not for delight ;
    Because with sudden motion from the ground
She raised her piercing orbs, and fill'd with light
    The interval of sound.

Still with their fires Love tipt his keenest darts ;
    As once they drew into two burning rings
All beams of Love, melting the mighty hearts
    Of captains and of kings.

Slowly my sense undazzled. Then I heard
    A noise of some one coming thro' the lawn,
And singing clearer than the crested bird
    That claps his wings at dawn.

' The torrent brooks of hallow'd Israel
    From craggy hollows pouring, late and soon,
Sound all night long, in falling thro' the dell,
    Far-heard beneath the moon.

' The balmy moon of blessed Israel
    Floods all the deep-blue gloom with beams divine :
All night the splinter'd crags that wall the dell
    With spires of silver shine.'

As one that museth where broad sunshine laves
    The lawn by some cathedral, thro' the door
Hearing the holy organ rolling waves
    Of sound on roof and floor

Within, and anthem sung, is charm'd and tied
    To where he stands,—so stood I, when that flow
Of music left the lips of her that died
    To save her father's vow ;

The daughter of the warrior Gileadite,
    A maiden pure ; as when she went along
From Mizpeh's tower'd gate with welcome light,
    With timbrel and with song.

My words leapt forth : ' Heaven heads the count of crimes
    With that wild oath.' She render'd answer high :
' Not so, nor once alone ; a thousand times
    I would be born and die.

'Single I grew, like some green plant, whose root
  Creeps to the garden water-pipes beneath,
Feeding the flower; but ere my flower to fruit
  Changed, I was ripe for death.

'My God, my land, my father—these did move
  Me from my bliss of life, that Nature gave,
Lower'd softly with a threefold cord of love
  Down to a silent grave.

'And I went mourning, "No fair Hebrew boy
  Shall smile away my maiden blame among
The Hebrew mothers"—emptied of all joy,
  Leaving the dance and song,

'Leaving the olive-gardens far below,
  Leaving the promise of my bridal bower,
The valleys of grape-loaded vines that glow
  Beneath the battled tower.

'The light white cloud swam over us. Anon
  We heard the lion roaring from his den;
We saw the large white stars rise one by one,
  Or, from the darken'd glen,

'Saw God divide the night with flying flame,
  And thunder on the everlasting hills.
I heard Him, for He spake, and grief became
  A solemn scorn of ills.

'When the next moon was roll'd into the sky,
  Strength came to me that equall'd my desire.
How beautiful a thing it was to die
  For God and for my sire!

'It comforts me in this one thought to dwell,
  That I subdued me to my father's will;
Because the kiss he gave me, ere I fell,
  Sweetens the spirit still.

'Moreover it is written that my race
  Hew'd Ammon, hip and thigh, from Aroer
On Arnon unto Minneth.' Here her face
  Glow'd, as I look'd at her.

She lock'd her lips: she left me where I stood:
   'Glory to God,' she sang, and past afar,
Thridding the sombre boskage of the wood,
   Toward the morning-star.

Losing her carol I stood pensively,
   As one that from a casement leans his head,
When midnight bells cease ringing suddenly,
   And the old year is dead.

'Alas! alas!' a low voice, full of care,
   Murmur'd beside me: 'Turn and look on me:
I am that Rosamond, whom men call fair,
   If what I was I be.

'Would I had been some maiden coarse and poor!
   O me, that I should ever see the light!
Those dragon eyes of anger'd Eleanòr
   Do hunt me, day and night.'

She ceased in tears, fallen from hope and trust:
   To whom the Egyptian: 'O, you tamely died!
You should have clung to Fulvia's waist, and thrust
   The dagger thro' her side.'

With that sharp sound the white dawn's creeping beams,
   Stol'n to my brain, dissolved the mystery
Of folded sleep. The captain of my dreams
   Ruled in the eastern sky.

Morn broaden'd on the borders of the dark,
   Ere I saw her, who clasp'd in her last trance
Her murder'd father's head, or Joan of Arc,
   A light of ancient France;

Or her who knew that Love can vanquish Death,
   Who kneeling, with one arm about her king,
Drew forth the poison with her balmy breath,
   Sweet as new buds in Spring.

No memory labours longer from the deep
   Gold-mines of thought to lift the hidden ore
That glimpses, moving up, than I from sleep
   To gather and tell o'er

Each little sound and sight. With what dull pain
    Compass'd, how eagerly I sought to strike
Into that wondrous track of dreams again!
    But no two dreams are like.

As when a soul laments, which hath been blest,
    Desiring what is mingled with past years,
In yearnings that can never be exprest
    By signs or groans or tears;

Because all words, tho' cull'd with choicest art,
    Failing to give the bitter of the sweet,
Wither beneath the palate, and the heart
    Faints, faded by its heat.

II

THE PALACE OF ART

I BUILT my soul a lordly pleasure-house,
    Wherein at ease for aye to dwell.
I said, 'O Soul, make merry and carouse,
    Dear soul, for all is well.'

A huge crag-platform, smooth as burnish'd brass
    I chose. The ranged ramparts bright
From level meadow-bases of deep grass
    Suddenly scaled the light.

Thereon I built it firm. Of ledge or shelf
    The rock rose clear, or winding stair.
My soul would live alone unto herself
    In her high palace there.

And 'while the world runs round and round,' I said,
    'Reign thou apart, a quiet king,
Still as, while Saturn whirls, his stedfast shade
    Sleeps on his luminous ring.'

To which my soul made answer readily:
    'Trust me, in bliss I shall abide
In this great mansion, that is built for me,
    So royal-rich and wide.'

* * * *
* * * *

Four courts I made, East, West and South and North,
    In each a squared lawn, wherefrom
The golden gorge of dragons spouted forth
    A flood of fountain-foam.

And round the cool green courts there ran a row
    Of cloisters, branch'd like mighty woods,
Echoing all night to that sonorous flow
    Of spouted fountain-floods.

And round the roofs a gilded gallery
    That lent broad verge to distant lands,
Far as the wild swan wings, to where the sky
    Dipt down to sea and sands.

From those four jets four currents in one swell
    Across the mountain stream'd below
In misty folds, that floating as they fell
    Lit up a torrent-bow.

And high on every peak a statue seem'd
    To hang on tiptoe, tossing up
A cloud of incense of all odour steam'd
    From out a golden cup.

So that she thought, 'And who shall gaze upon
    My palace with unblinded eyes,
While this great bow will waver in the sun,
    And that sweet incense rise?'

For that sweet incense rose and never fail'd,
    And, while day sank or mounted higher,
The light aërial gallery, golden-rail'd,
    Burnt like a fringe of fire.

Likewise the deep-set windows, stain'd and traced,
    Would seem slow-flaming crimson fires
From shadow'd grots of arches interlaced,
    And tipt with frost-like spires.

* * * *
* * * *

The Palace of Art

Full of long-sounding corridors it was,
    That over-vaulted grateful gloom,
Thro' which the livelong day my soul did pass,
    Well-pleased, from room to room.

Full of great rooms and small the palace stood,
    All various, each a perfect whole
From living Nature, fit for every mood
    And change of my still soul.

For some were hung with arras green and blue,
    Showing a gaudy summer-morn,
Where with puff'd cheek the belted hunter blew
    His wreathed bugle-horn.

One seem'd all dark and red—a tract of sand,
    And some one pacing there alone,
Who paced for ever in a glimmering land,
    Lit with a low large moon.

One show'd an iron coast and angry waves.
    You seem'd to hear them climb and fall
And roar rock-thwarted under bellowing caves,
    Beneath the windy wall.

And one, a full-fed river winding slow
    By herds upon an endless plain,
The ragged rims of thunder brooding low,
    With shadow-streaks of rain.

And one, the reapers at their sultry toil.
    In front they bound the sheaves. Behind
Were realms of upland, prodigal in oil,
    And hoary to the wind.

And one a foreground black with stones and slags,
    Beyond, a line of heights, and higher
All barr'd with long white cloud the scornful crags,
    And highest, snow and fire.

And one, an English home—gray twilight pour'd
    On dewy pastures, dewy trees,
Softer than sleep—all things in order stored,
    A haunt of ancient Peace.

Nor these alone, but every landscape fair,
  As fit for every mood of mind,
Or gay, or grave, or sweet, or stern, was there
  Not less than truth design'd.

*   *   *   *
*   *   *   *

Or the maid-mother by a crucifix,
  In tracts of pasture sunny-warm,
Beneath branch-work of costly sardonyx
  Sat smiling, babe in arm.

Or in a clear-wall'd city on the sea,
  Near gilded organ-pipes, her hair
Wound with white roses, slept St. Cecily;
  An angel look'd at her.

Or thronging all one porch of Paradise
  A group of Houris bow'd to see
The dying Islamite, with hands and eyes
  That said, We wait for thee.

Or mythic Uther's deeply-wounded son
  In some fair space of sloping greens
Lay, dozing in the vale of Avalon,
  And watch'd by weeping queens.

Or hollowing one hand against his ear,
  To list a foot-fall, ere he saw
The wood-nymph, stay'd the Ausonian king to hear
  Of wisdom and of law.

Or over hills with peaky tops engrail'd,
  And many a tract of palm and rice,
The throne of Indian Cama slowly sail'd
  A summer fann'd with spice.

Or sweet Europa's mantle blew unclasp'd,
  From off her shoulder backward borne:
From one hand droop'd a crocus: one hand grasp'd
  The mild bull's golden horn.

Or else flush'd Ganymede, his rosy thigh
  Half-buried in the Eagle's down,
Sole as a flying star shot thro' the sky
  Above the pillar'd town.

Nor these alone: but every legend fair
  Which the supreme Caucasian mind
Carved out of Nature for itself, was there,
  Not less than life, design'd.

    *   *   *   *
    *   *   *   *

Then in the towers I placed great bells that swung,
  Moved of themselves, with silver sound;
And with choice paintings of wise men I hung
  The royal dais round.

For there was Milton like a seraph strong,
  Beside him Shakespeare bland and mild;
And there the world-worn Dante grasp'd his song,
  And somewhat grimly smiled.

And there the Ionian father of the rest;
  A million wrinkles carved his skin;
A hundred winters snow'd upon his breast,
  From cheek and throat and chin.

Above, the fair hall-ceiling stately-set
  Many an arch high up did lift,
And angels rising and descending met
  With interchange of gift.

Below was all mosaic choicely plann'd
  With cycles of the human tale
Of this wide world, the times of every land
  So wrought, they will not fail.

The people here, a beast of burden slow,
  Toil'd onward, prick'd with goads and stings;
Here play'd, a tiger, rolling to and fro
  The heads and crowns of kings;

Here rose, an athlete, strong to break or bind
    All force in bonds that might endure,
And here once more like some sick man declined,
    And trusted any cure.

But over these she trod : and those great bells
    Began to chime. She took her throne :
She sat betwixt the shining Oriels,
    To sing her songs alone.

And thro' the topmost Oriels' coloured flame
    Two godlike faces gazed below ;
Plato the wise, and large-brow'd Verulam,
    The first of those who know.

And all those names, that in their motion were
    Full-welling fountain-heads of change,
Betwixt the slender shafts were blazon'd fair
    In diverse raiment strange :

Thro' which the lights, rose, amber, emerald, blue,
    Flush'd in her temples and her eyes,
And from her lips, as morn from Memnon, drew
    Rivers of melodies.

No nightingale delighteth to prolong
    Her low preamble all alone,
More than my soul to hear her echo'd song
    Throb thro' the ribbed stone ;

Singing and murmuring in her feastful mirth,
    Joying to feel herself alive,
Lord over Nature, Lord of the visible earth,
    Lord of the senses five ;

Communing with herself : 'All these are mine,
    And let the world have peace or wars,
'Tis one to me.' She—when young night divine
    Crown'd dying day with stars,

Making sweet close of his delicious toils—
    Lit light in wreaths and anadems,
And pure quintessences of precious oils
    In hollow'd moons of gems,

The Palace of Art

To mimic heaven; and clapt her hands and cried,
  'I marvel if my still delight
In this great house so royal-rich, and wide,
  Be flatter'd to the height.

'O all things fair to sate my various eyes!
  O shapes and hues that please me well!
O silent faces of the Great and Wise,
  My Gods, with whom I dwell!

'O God-like isolation which art mine,
  I can but count thee perfect gain,
What time I watch the darkening droves of swine
  That range on yonder plain.

'In filthy sloughs they roll a prurient skin,
  They graze and wallow, breed and sleep;
And oft some brainless devil enters in,
  And drives them to the deep.'

Then of the moral instinct would she prate
  And of the rising from the dead,
As hers by right of full-accomplish'd Fate;
  And at the last she said:

'I take possession of man's mind and deed.
  I care not what the sects may brawl.
I sit as God holding no form of creed,
  But contemplating all.'

*   *   *   *
*   *   *   *

Full oft the riddle of the painful earth
  Flash'd thro' her as she sat alone,
Yet not the less held she her solemn mirth,
  And intellectual throne.

And so she throve and prosper'd: so three years
  She prosper'd: on the fourth she fell,
Like Herod, when the shout was in his ears,
  Struck thro' with pangs of hell.

Lest she should fail and perish utterly,
  God, before whom ever lie bare
The abysmal deeps of Personality,
    Plagued her with sore despair.

When she would think, where'er she turn'd her sight
  The airy hand confusion wrought,
Wrote, 'Mene, mene,' and divided quite
    The kingdom of her thought.

Deep dread and loathing of her solitude
  Fell on her, from which mood was born
Scorn of herself; again, from out that mood
    Laughter at her self-scorn.

'What! is not this my place of strength,' she said,
  'My spacious mansion built for me,
Whereof the strong foundation-stones were laid
    Since my first memory?'

But in dark corners of her palace stood
  Uncertain shapes; and unawares
On white-eyed phantasms weeping tears of blood,
    And horrible nightmares,

And hollow shades enclosing hearts of flame,
  And, with dim fretted foreheads all,
On corpses three-months-old at noon she came,
    That stood against the wall.

A spot of dull stagnation, without light
  Or power of movement, seem'd my soul,
'Mid onward-sloping motions infinite
    Making for one sure goal.

A still salt pool, lock'd in with bars of sand,
  Left on the shore; that hears all night
The plunging seas draw backward from the land
    Their moon-led waters white.

A star that with the choral starry dance
  Join'd not, but stood, and standing saw
The hollow orb of moving Circumstance
    Roll'd round by one fix'd law.

Back on herself her serpent pride had curl'd.
 'No voice,' she shriek'd in that lone hall,
'No voice breaks thro' the stillness of this world:
 One deep, deep silence all!'

She, mouldering with the dull earth's mouldering sod,
 Inwrapt tenfold in slothful shame,
Lay there exiled from eternal God,
 Lost to her place and name;

And death and life she hated equally,
 And nothing saw, for her despair,
But dreadful time, dreadful eternity,
 No comfort anywhere;

Remaining utterly confused with fears,
 And ever worse with growing time,
And ever unrelieved by dismal tears,
 And all alone in crime:

Shut up as in a crumbling tomb, girt round
 With blackness as a solid wall,
Far off she seem'd to hear the dully sound
 Of human footsteps fall.

As in strange lands a traveller walking slow,
 In doubt and great perplexity,
A little before moon-rise hears the low
 Moan of an unknown sea;

And knows not if it be thunder, or a sound
 Of rocks thrown down, or one deep cry
Of great wild beasts; then thinketh, 'I have found
 A new land, but I die.'

She howl'd aloud, 'I am on fire within.
 There comes no murmur of reply.
What is it that will take away my sin,
 And save me lest I die?'

So when four years were wholly finished,
 She threw her royal robes away.
'Make me a cottage in the vale,' she said,
 'Where I may mourn and pray.

'Yet pull not down my palace towers, that are
    So lightly, beautifully built :
Perchance I may return with others there
    When I have purged my guilt.'

III

LOCKSLEY HALL

COMRADES, leave me here a little, while as yet 'tis early morn :
Leave me here, and when you want me, sound upon the bugle-horn.

'Tis the place, and all around it, as of old, the curlews call,
Dreary gleams about the moorland flying over Locksley Hall ;

Locksley Hall, that in the distance overlooks the sandy tracts,
And the hollow ocean-ridges roaring into cataracts.

Many a night from yonder ivied casement, ere I went to rest,
Did I look on great Orion sloping slowly to the West.

Many a night I saw the Pleiads, rising thro' the mellow shade,
Glitter like a swarm of fire-flies tangled in a silver braid.

Here about the beach I wander'd, nourishing a youth sublime
With the fairy tales of science, and the long result of Time ;

When the centuries behind me like a fruitful land reposed ;
When I clung to all the present for the promise that it closed :

When I dipt into the future far as human eye could see;
Saw the Vision of the world, and all the wonder that would be.——

In the Spring a fuller crimson comes upon the robin's breast;
In the Spring the wanton lapwing gets himself another crest;

In the Spring a livelier iris changes on the burnish'd dove;
In the Spring a young man's fancy lightly turns to thoughts of love.

Then her cheek was pale and thinner than should be for one so young,
And her eyes on all my motions with a mute observance hung.

And I said, 'My cousin Amy, speak, and speak the truth to me,
Trust me, cousin, all the current of my being sets to thee.'

On her pallid cheek and forehead came a colour and a light,
As I have seen the rosy red flushing in the northern night.

And she turn'd—her bosom shaken with a sudden storm of sighs—
All the spirit deeply dawning in the dark of hazel eyes—

Saying, 'I have hid my feelings, fearing they should do me wrong;'
Saying, 'Dost thou love me, cousin?' weeping, 'I have loved thee long.'

Love took up the glass of Time, and turn'd it in his glowing hands;
Every moment, lightly shaken, ran itself in golden sands.

Love took up the harp of Life, and smote on all the chords with might ;
Smote the chord of Self, that, trembling, pass'd in music out of sight.

Many a morning on the moorland did we hear the copses ring,
And her whisper throng'd my pulses with the fulness of the Spring.

Many an evening by the waters did we watch the stately ships,
And our spirits rush'd together at the touching of the lips.

O my cousin, shallow-hearted! O my Amy, mine no more!
O the dreary, dreary moorland! O the barren, barren shore!

Falser than all fancy fathoms, falser than all songs have sung,
Puppet to a father's threat, and servile to a shrewish tongue!

Is it well to wish thee happy?—having known me— to decline
On a range of lower feelings and a narrower heart than mine!

Yet it shall be: thou shalt lower to his level day by day,
What is fine within thee growing coarse to sympathise with clay.

As the husband is, the wife is: thou art mated with a clown,
And the grossness of his nature will have weight to drag thee down.

He will hold thee, when his passion shall have spent its novel force,
Something better than his dog, a little dearer than his horse.

What is this? his eyes are heavy: think not they are glazed with wine.
Go to him: it is thy duty: kiss him: take his hand in thine.

It may be my lord is weary, that his brain is overwrought:
Soothe him with thy finer fancies, touch him with thy lighter thought.

He will answer to the purpose, easy things to understand—
Better thou wert dead before me, tho' I slew thee with my hand!

Better thou and I were lying, hidden from the heart's disgrace,
Roll'd in one another's arms, and silent in a last embrace.

Cursed be the social wants that sin against the strength of youth!
Cursed be the social lies that warp us from the living truth!

Cursed be the sickly forms that err from honest Nature's rule!
Cursed be the gold that gilds the straiten'd forehead of the fool!

Well—'tis well that I should bluster!—Hadst thou less unworthy proved—
Would to God—for I had loved thee more than ever wife was loved.

Am I mad, that I should cherish that which bears but bitter fruit?
I will pluck it from my bosom, tho' my heart be at the root.

Never, tho' my mortal summers to such length of years should come
As the many-winter'd crow that leads the clanging rookery home.

Where is comfort? in division of the records of the mind?
Can I part her from herself, and love her, as I knew her, kind?

I remember one that perish'd: sweetly did she speak and move:
Such a one do I remember, whom to look at was to love.

Can I think of her as dead, and love her for the love she bore?
No—she never loved me truly: love is love for evermore.

Comfort? comfort scorn'd of devils! this is truth the poet sings,
That a sorrow's crown of sorrow is remembering happier things.

Drug thy memories, lest thou learn it, lest thy heart be put to proof,
In the dead unhappy night, and when the rain is on the roof.

Like a dog, he hunts in dreams, and thou art staring at the wall,
Where the dying night-lamp flickers, and the shadows rise and fall.

Then a hand shall pass before thee, pointing to his drunken sleep,
To thy widow'd marriage-pillows, to the tears that thou wilt weep.

Thou shalt hear the 'Never, never,' whisper'd by the phantom years,
And a song from out the distance in the ringing of thine ears;

And an eye shall vex thee, looking ancient kindness on thy pain.
Turn thee, turn thee on thy pillow: get thee to thy rest again.

Nay, but Nature brings thee solace; for a tender
   voice will cry.
'Tis a purer life than thine; a lip to drain thy trouble
   dry.

Baby lips will laugh me down: my latest rival brings
   thee rest.
Baby fingers, waxen touches, press me from the
   mother's breast.

O, the child too clothes the father with a dearness
   not his due.
Half is thine and half is his: it will be worthy of the
   two.

O, I see thee old and formal, fitted to thy petty part,
With a little hoard of maxims preaching down a
   daughter's heart.

'They were dangerous guides the feelings—she herself
   was not exempt—
Truly, she herself had suffer'd'—Perish in thy self-
   contempt!

Overlive it—lower yet—be happy! wherefore should
   I care?
I myself must mix with action, lest I wither by despair.

What is that which I should turn to, lighting upon
   days like these?
Every door is barr'd with gold, and opens but to
   golden keys.

Every gate is throng'd with suitors, all the markets
   overflow.
I have but an angry fancy: what is that which I
   should do?

I had been content to perish, falling on the foeman's
   ground,
When the ranks are roll'd in vapour, and the winds
   are laid with sound.

But the jingling of the guinea helps the hurt that Honour feels,
And the nations do but murmur, snarling at each other's heels.

Can I but relive in sadness? I will turn that earlier page.
Hide me from my deep emotion, O thou wondrous Mother-Age!

Make me feel the wild pulsation that I felt before the strife,
When I heard my days before me, and the tumult of my life;

Yearning for the large excitement that the coming years would yield,
Eager-hearted as a boy when first he leaves his father's field,

And at night along the dusky highway near and nearer drawn,
Sees in heaven the light of London flaring like a dreary dawn;

And his spirit leaps within him to be gone before him then,
Underneath the light he looks at, in among the throngs of men:

Men, my brothers, men the workers, ever reaping something new:
That which they have done but earnest of the things that they shall do:

For I dipt into the future, far as human eye could see,
Saw the Vision of the world, and all the wonder that would be;

Saw the heavens fill with commerce, argosies of magic sails,
Pilots of the purple twilight, dropping down with costly bales;

Heard the heavens fill with shouting, and there rain'd
   a ghastly dew
From the nations' airy navies grappling in the central
   blue;

Far along the world-wide whisper of the south-wind
   rushing warm,
With the standards of the peoples plunging thro' the
   thunder-storm;

Till the war-drum throbb'd no longer, and the battle-
   flags were furl'd
In the Parliament of man, the Federation of the world.

There the common sense of most shall hold a fretful
   realm in awe,
And the kindly earth shall slumber, lapt in universal
   law.

So I triumph'd ere my passion sweeping thro' me left
   me dry,
Left me with the palsied heart, and left me with the
   jaundiced eye;

Eye, to which all order festers, all things here are out
   of joint:
Science moves, but slowly slowly, creeping on from
   point to point:

Slowly comes a hungry people, as a lion creeping
   nigher,
Glares at one that nods and winks behind a slowly
   dying fire.

Yet I doubt not thro' the ages one increasing purpose
   runs,
And the thoughts of men are widen'd with the process
   of the suns.

What is that to him that reaps not harvest of his youthful joys,
Tho' the deep heart of existence beat for ever like a
   boy's?

Knowledge comes, but wisdom lingers, and I linger on the shore,
And the individual withers, and the world is more and more.

Knowledge comes, but wisdom lingers, and he bears a laden breast,
Full of sad experience, moving toward the stillness of his rest.

Hark, my merry comrades call me, sounding on the bugle-horn,
They to whom my foolish passion were a target for their scorn:

Shall it not be scorn to me to harp on such a moulder'd string?
I am shamed thro' all my nature to have loved so slight a thing.

Weakness to be wroth with weakness! woman's pleasure, woman's pain—
Nature made them blinder motions bounded in a shallower brain:

Woman is the lesser man, and all thy passions, match'd with mine,
Are as moonlight unto sunlight, and as water unto wine—

Here at least, where nature sickens, nothing. Ah, for some retreat
Deep in yonder shining Orient, where my life began to beat;

Where in wild Mahratta-battle fell my father evil-starr'd;—
I was left a trampled orphan, and a selfish uncle's ward.

Or to burst all links of habit—there to wander far away,
On from island unto island at the gateways of the day.

Larger constellations burning, mellow moons and happy skies,
Breadths of tropic shade and palms in cluster, knots of Paradise.

Never comes the trader, never floats an European flag,
Slides the bird o'er lustrous woodland, swings the trailer from the crag;

Droops the heavy-blossom'd bower, hangs the heavy-fruited tree—
Summer isles of Eden lying in dark-purple spheres of sea.

There methinks would be enjoyment more than in this march of mind,
In the steamship, in the railway, in the thoughts that shake mankind.

There the passions cramp'd no longer shall have scope and breathing space;
I will take some savage woman, she shall rear my dusky race.

Iron jointed, supple-sinew'd, they shall dive, and they shall run,
Catch the wild goat by the hair, and hurl their lances in the sun;

Whistle back the parrot's call, and leap the rainbows of the brooks,
Not with blinded eyesight poring over miserable books—

Fool, again the dream, the fancy! but I *know* my words are wild,
But I count the gray barbarian lower than the Christian child.

I, to herd with narrow foreheads, vacant of our glorious gains,
Like a beast with lower pleasures, like a beast with lower pains!

Mated with a squalid savage—what to me were sun
or clime?
I the heir of all the ages, in the foremost files of
time—

I that rather held it better men should perish one by
one,
Than that earth should stand at gaze like Joshua's
moon in Ajalon!

Not in vain the distance beacons. Forward, forward
let us range,
Let the great world spin for ever down the ringing
grooves of change.

Thro' the shadow of the globe we sweep into the
younger day:
Better fifty years of Europe than a cycle of Cathay.

Mother-Age (for mine I knew not) help me as when
life begun:
Rift the hills, and roll the waters, flash the lightnings,
weigh the Sun.

O, I see the crescent promise of my spirit hath not
set.
Ancient founts of inspiration well thro' all my fancy
yet.

Howsoever these things be, a long farewell to Locksley
Hall!
Now for me the woods may wither, now for me the
roof-tree fall.

Comes a vapour from the margin, blackening over
heath and holt,
Cramming all the blast before it, in its breast a
thunderbolt.

Let it fall on Locksley Hall, with rain or hail, or fire
or snow;
For the mighty wind arises, roaring seaward, and
I go.

IV

THE MAY QUEEN

You must wake and call me early, call me early, mother dear;
To-morrow 'ill be the happiest time of all the glad New-year;
Of all the glad New-year, mother, the maddest merriest day;
For I'm to be Queen o' the May, mother, I'm to be Queen o' the May.

There's many a black black eye, they say, but none so bright as mine;
There's Margaret and Mary, there's Kate and Caroline:
But none so fair as little Alice in all the land they say,
So I'm to be Queen o' the May, mother, I'm to be Queen o' the May.

I sleep so sound all night, mother, that I shall never wake,
If you do not call me loud when the day begins to break:
But I must gather knots of flowers, and buds and garlands gay,
For I'm to be Queen o' the May, mother, I'm to be Queen o' the May.

As I came up the valley whom think ye should I see,
But Robin leaning on the bridge beneath the hazel-tree?
He thought of that sharp look, mother, I gave him yesterday,
But I'm to be Queen o' the May, mother, I'm to be Queen o' the May.

He thought I was a ghost, mother, for I was all in white,
And I ran by him without speaking, like a flash of light.
They call me cruel-hearted, but I care not what they say,
For I'm to be Queen o' the May, mother, I'm to be Queen o' the May.

They say he's dying all for love, but that can never be:
They say his heart is breaking, mother—what is that
   to me?
There's many a bolder lad 'ill woo me any summer
   day,
And I'm to be Queen o' the May, mother, I'm to be
   Queen o' the May.

Little Effie shall go with me to-morrow to the green,
And you'll be there, too, mother, to see me made the
   Queen;
For the shepherd lads on every side 'ill come from far
   away,
And I'm to be Queen o' the May, mother, I'm to be
   Queen o' the May.

The honeysuckle round the porch has wov'n its wavy
   bowers,
And by the meadow-trenches blow the faint sweet
   cuckoo-flowers;
And the wild marsh-marigold shines like fire in
   swamps and hollows gray,
And I'm to be Queen o' the May, mother, I'm to be
   Queen o' the May.

The night-winds come and go, mother, upon the
   meadow-grass,
And the happy stars above them seem to brighten as
   they pass;
There will not be a drop of rain the whole of the live-
   long day,
And I'm to be Queen o' the May, mother, I'm to be
   Queen o' the May.

All the valley, mother, 'ill be fresh and green and
   still,
And the cowslip and the crowfoot are over all the
   hill,
And the rivulet in the flowery dale 'ill merrily glance
   and play,
For I'm to be Queen o' the May, mother, I'm to be
   Queen o' the May.

So you must wake and call me early, call me early, mother dear,
To-morrow 'ill be the happiest time of all the glad New-year :
To-morrow 'ill be of all the year the maddest merriest day,
For I'm to be Queen o' the May, mother, I'm to be Queen o' the May.

NEW-YEAR'S EVE

IF you're waking call me early, call me early, mother dear,
For I would see the sun rise upon the glad New-year.
It is the last New-year that I shall ever see,
Then you may lay me low i' the mould and think no more of me.

To-night I saw the sun set : he set and left behind
The good old year, the dear old time, and all my peace of mind ;
And the New-year's coming up, mother, but I shall never see
The blossom on the blackthorn, the leaf upon the tree.

Last May we made a crown of flowers : we had a merry day ;
Beneath the hawthorn on the green they made me Queen of May ;
And we danced about the may-pole and in the hazel copse,
Till Charles's Wain came out above the tall white chimney-tops.

There's not a flower on all the hills : the frost is on the pane :
I only wish to live till the snowdrops come again :
I wish the snow would melt and the sun come out on high :
I long to see a flower so before the day I die.

The building rook 'ill caw from the windy tall elm-tree,
And the tufted plover pipe along the fallow lea,
And the swallow 'ill come back again with summer
   o'er the wave,
But I shall lie alone, mother, within the mouldering
   grave.

Upon the chancel-casement, and upon that grave of
   mine,
In the early early morning the summer sun 'ill shine,
Before the red cock crows from the farm upon the hill,
When you are warm-asleep, mother, and all the world
   is still.

When the flowers come again, mother, beneath the
   waning light
You'll never see me more in the long gray fields at
   night ;
When from the dry dark wold the summer airs blow
   cool
On the oat-grass and the sword-grass, and the bulrush
   in the pool.

You'll bury me, my mother, just beneath the hawthorn shade,
And you'll come sometimes and see me where I am
   lowly laid.
I shall not forget you, mother, I shall hear you when
   you pass,
With your feet above my head in the long and pleasant grass.

I have been wild and wayward, but you'll forgive me
   now ;
You'll kiss me, my own mother, and forgive me ere I go ;
Nay, nay, you must not weep, nor let your grief be wild,
You should not fret for me, mother, you have another
   child.

If I can I'll come again, mother, from out my resting-
   place ;
Tho' you'll not see me, mother, I shall look upon
   your face ;

Tho' I cannot speak a word, I shall harken what you say,
And be often, often with you when you think I'm far away.

Goodnight, goodnight, when I have said goodnight for evermore,
And you see me carried out from the threshold of the door;
Don't let Effie come to see me till my grave be growing green:
She'll be a better child to you than ever I have been.

She'll find my garden-tools upon the granary floor:
Let her take 'em: they are hers: I shall never garden more:
But tell her, when I'm gone, to train the rosebush that I set
About the parlour-window and the box of mignonette.

Goodnight, sweet mother: call me before the day is born.
All night I lie awake, but I fall asleep at morn;
But I would see the sun rise upon the glad New-year,
So, if you're waking call me, call me early, mother dear.

CONCLUSION

I THOUGHT to pass away before, and yet alive I am;
And in the fields all round I hear the bleating of the lamb.
How sadly, I remember, rose the morning of the year!
To die before the snowdrop came, and now the violet's here.

O sweet is the new violet, that comes beneath the skies,
And sweeter is the young lamb's voice to me that cannot rise,
And sweet is all the land about, and all the flowers that blow,
And sweeter far is death than life to me that long to go.

It seem'd so hard at first, mother, to leave the blessed sun,
And now it seems as hard to stay, and yet His will be done!
But still I think it can't be long before I find release;
And that good man, the clergyman, has told me words of peace.

O blessings on his kindly voice and on his silver hair!
And blessings on his whole life long, until he meet me there!
O blessings on his kindly heart and on his silver head!
A thousand times I blest him, as he knelt beside my bed.

He taught me all the mercy, for he show'd me all the sin.
Now, tho' my lamp was lighted late, there's One will let me in:
Nor would I now be well, mother, again if that could be,
For my desire is but to pass to Him that died for me.

I did not hear the dog howl, mother, or the death-watch beat,
There came a sweeter token when the night and morning meet:
But sit beside my bed, mother, and put your hand in mine,
And Effie on the other side, and I will tell the sign.

All in the wild March-morning I heard the angels call;
It was when the moon was setting, and the dark was over all;
The trees began to whisper, and the wind began to roll,
And in the wild March-morning I heard them call my soul.

For lying broad awake I thought of you and Effie dear;
I saw you sitting in the house, and I no longer here;
With all my strength I pray'd for both, and so I felt resign'd,
And up the valley came a swell of music on the wind.

I thought that it was fancy, and I listen'd in my bed,
And then did something speak to me—I know not what was said;

For great delight and shuddering took hold of all my
    mind,
And up the valley came again the music on the wind.

But you were sleeping; and I said, 'It's not for them:
    it's mine.'
And if it come three times, I thought, I take it for a
    sign.
And once again it came, and close beside the window-
    bars,
Then seem'd to go right up to Heaven and die among
    the stars.

So now I think my time is near. I trust it is. I know
The blessed music went that way my soul will have
    to go.
And for myself, indeed, I care not if I go to-day.
But, Effie, you must comfort *her* when I am past away.

And say to Robin a kind word, and tell him not to fret;
There's many a worthier than I, would make him
    happy yet.
If I had lived—I cannot tell—I might have been his
    wife;
But all these things have ceased to be, with my desire
    of life.

O look! the sun begins to rise, the heavens are in a
    glow;
He shines upon a hundred fields, and all of them I
    know.
And there I move no longer now, and there his light
    may shine—
Wild flowers in the valley for other hands than mine.

O sweet and strange it seems to me, that ere this day
    is done
The voice, that now is speaking, may be beyond the
    sun—
For ever and for ever with those just souls and true—
And what is life, that we should moan? why make
    we such ado?

For ever and for ever, all in a blessed home—
And there to wait a little while till you and Effie come—
To lie within the light of God, as I lie upon your breast—
And the wicked cease from troubling, and the weary are at rest.

V

IN THE CHILDREN'S HOSPITAL

EMMIE

I

Our doctor had call'd in another, I never had seen him before,
But he sent a chill to my heart when I saw him come in at the door,
Fresh from the surgery-schools of France and of other lands—
Harsh red hair, big voice, big chest, big merciless hands!
Wonderful cures he had done, O yes, but they said too of him
He was happier using the knife than in trying to save the limb,
And that I can well believe, for he look'd so coarse and so red,—
I could think he was one of those who would break their jests on the dead,
And mangle the living dog that had loved him and fawn'd at his knee—
Drench'd with the hellish oorali—that ever such things should be!

II

Here was a boy—I am sure that some of our children would die
But for the voice of Love, and the smile, and the comforting eye—

Here was a boy in the ward, every bone seem'd out
    of its place—
Caught in a mill and crush'd—it was all but a hope-
    less case:
And he handled him gently enough; but his voice
    and his face were not kind,
And it was but a hopeless case, he had seen it and
    made up his mind,
And he said to me roughly 'The lad will need little
    more of your care.'
'All the more need,' I told him, 'to seek the Lord
    Jesus in prayer;
They are all his children here, and I pray for them
    all as my own:'
But he turn'd to me, 'Ay, good woman, can prayer
    set a broken bone?'
Then he mutter'd half to himself, but I know that I
    heard him say
'All very well—but the good Lord Jesus has had his
    day.'

III

Had? has it come? It has only dawn'd. It will
    come by and by.
O how could I serve in the wards if the hope of the
    world were a lie?
How could I bear with the sights and the loathsome
    smells of disease
But that He said 'Ye do it to me, when ye do it to
    these'?

IV

So he went. And we past to this ward where the
    younger children are laid:
Here is the cot of our orphan, our darling, our meek
    little maid;
Empty you see just now! We have lost her who
    loved her so much—
Patient of pain tho' as quick as a sensitive plant to
    the touch;

Hers was the prettiest prattle, it often moved me to tears,
Hers was the gratefullest heart I have found in a child of her years—
Nay you remember our Emmie; you used to send her the flowers;
How she would smile at 'em, play with 'em, talk to 'em hours after hours!
They that can wander at will where the works of the Lord are reveal'd
Little guess what joy can be got from a cowslip out of the field;
Flowers to these 'spirits in prison' are all they can know of the spring,
They freshen and sweeten the wards like the waft of an Angel's wing;
And she lay with a flower in one hand and her thin hands crost on her breast—
Wan, but as pretty as heart can desire, and we thought her at rest,
Quietly sleeping—so quiet, our doctor said 'Poor little dear,
Nurse, I must do it to-morrow; she'll never live thro' it, I fear.'

V

I walk'd with our kindly old doctor as far as the head of the stair,
Then I return'd to the ward; the child didn't see I was there.

VI

Never since I was nurse, had I been so grieved and so vext!
Emmie had heard him. Softly she call'd from her cot to the next,
'He says I shall never live thro' it, O Annie, what shall I do?'
Annie consider'd. 'If I,' said the wise little Annie, 'was you,

I should cry to the dear Lord Jesus to help me, for, Emmie, you see,
It's all in the picture there: "Little children should come to me."'
(Meaning the print that you gave us, I find that it always can please
Our children, the dear Lord Jesus with children about his knees.)
'Yes, and I will,' said Emmie, 'but then if I call to the Lord,
How should he know that it's me? such a lot of beds in the ward!'
That was a puzzle for Annie. Again she consider'd and said:
'Emmie, you put out your arms, and you leave 'em outside on the bed—
The Lord has so *much* to see to! but, Emmie, you tell it him plain,
It's the little girl with her arms lying out on the counterpane.'

VII

I had sat three nights by the child—I could not watch her for four—
My brain had begun to reel—I felt I could do it no more.
That was my sleeping-night, but I thought that it never would pass.
There was a thunderclap once, and a clatter of hail on the glass,
And there was a phantom cry that I heard as I tost about,
The motherless bleat of a lamb in the storm and the darkness without;
My sleep was broken besides with dreams of the dreadful knife
And fears for our delicate Emmie who scarce would escape with her life;
Then in the gray of the morning it seem'd she stood by me and smiled,
And the doctor came at his hour, and we went to see to the child.

VIII

He had brought his ghastly tools: we believed her asleep again—
Her dear, long, lean, little arms lying out on the counterpane;
Say that His day is done! Ah why should we care what they say?
The Lord of the children had heard her, and Emmie had past away.

VI

THE GRANDMOTHER

I

And Willy, my eldest-born, is gone, you say, little Anne?
Ruddy and white, and strong on his legs, he looks like a man.
And Willy's wife has written: she never was over-wise,
Never the wife for Willy: he wouldn't take my advice.

II

For, Annie, you see, her father was not the man to save,
Hadn't a head to manage, and drank himself into his grave.
Pretty enough, very pretty! but I was against it for one.
Eh!—but he wouldn't hear me—and Willy, you say, is gone.

III

Willy, my beauty, my eldest-born, the flower of the flock;
Never a man could fling him: for Willy stood like a rock.
'Here's a leg for a babe of a week!' says doctor; and he would be bound,
There was not his like that year in twenty parishes round.

IV

Strong of his hands, and strong on his legs, but still
    of his tongue!
I ought to have gone before him: I wonder he went
    so young.
I cannot cry for him, Annie: I have not long to stay;
Perhaps I shall see him the sooner, for he lived far away.

V

Why do you look at me, Annie? you think I am hard
    and cold;
But all my children have gone before me, I am so old:
I cannot weep for Willy, nor can I weep for the rest;
Only at your age, Annie, I could have wept with the
    best.

VI

For I remember a quarrel I had with your father, my
    dear,
All for a slanderous story, that cost me many a tear.
I mean your grandfather, Annie: it cost me a world
    of woe,
Seventy years ago, my darling, seventy years ago.

VII

For Jenny, my cousin, had come to the place, and I
    knew right well
That Jenny had tript in her time: I knew, but I would
    not tell.
And she to be coming and slandering me, the base
    little liar!
But the tongue is a fire as you know, my dear, the
    tongue is a fire.

VIII

And the parson made it his text that week, and he
    said likewise,
That a lie which is half a truth is ever the blackest of
    lies,

That a lie which is all a lie may be met and fought with outright,
But a lie which is part a truth is a harder matter to fight.

IX

And Willy had not been down to the farm for a week and a day;
And all things look'd half-dead, tho' it was the middle of May.
Jenny, to slander me, who knew what Jenny had been!
But soiling another, Annie, will never make oneself clean.

X

And I cried myself well-nigh blind, and all of an evening late
I climb'd to the top of the garth, and stood by the road at the gate.
The moon like a rick on fire was rising over the dale,
And whit, whit, whit, in the bush beside me chirrupt the nightingale.

XI

All of a sudden he stopt: there past by the gate of the farm,
Willy,—he didn't see me,—and Jenny hung on his arm.
Out into the road I started, and spoke I scarce knew how;
Ah, there's no fool like the old one—it makes me angry now.

XII

Willy stood up like a man, and look'd the thing that he meant;
Jenny, the viper, made me a mocking curtsey and went.
And I said, 'Let us part: in a hundred years it'll all be the same,
You cannot love me at all, if you love not my good name.'

XIII

And he turn'd, and I saw his eyes all wet, in the sweet moonshine :
'Sweetheart, I love you so well that your good name is mine.
And what do I care for Jane, let her speak of you well or ill ;
But marry me out of hand : we two shall be happy still.'

XIV

'Marry you, Willy !' said I, 'but I needs must speak my mind,
And I fear you'll listen to tales, be jealous and hard and unkind.'
But he turn'd and claspt me in his arms, and answer'd, 'No, love, no ;'
Seventy years ago, my darling, seventy years ago.

XV

So Willy and I were wedded : I wore a lilac gown ;
And the ringers rang with a will, and he gave the ringers a crown.
But the first that ever I bare was dead before he was born,
Shadow and shine is life, little Annie, flower and thorn.

XVI

That was the first time, too, that ever I thought of death.
There lay the sweet little body that never had drawn a breath.
I had not wept, little Anne, not since I had been a wife ;
But I wept like a child that day, for the babe had fought for his life.

XVII

His dear little face was troubled, as if with anger or
  pain :
I look'd at the still little body—his trouble had all
  been in vain.
For Willy I cannot weep, I shall see him another
  morn :
But I wept like a child for the child that was dead
  before he was born.

XVIII

But he cheer'd me, my good man, for he seldom said
  me nay :
Kind, like a man, was he ; like a man, too, would
  have his way :
Never jealous—not he : we had many a happy year ;
And he died, and I could not weep—my own time
  seem'd so near.

XIX

But I wish'd it had been God's will that I, too, then
  could have died :
I began to be tired a little, and fain had slept at his
  side.
And that was ten years back, or more, if I don't
  forget :
But as to the children, Annie, they're all about me yet.

XX

Pattering over the boards, my Annie who left me at
  two,
Patter she goes, my own little Annie, an Annie like
  you :
Pattering over the boards, she comes and goes at her
  will,
While Harry is in the five-acre and Charlie ploughing
  the hill.

XXI

And Harry and Charlie, I hear them too—they sing
    to their team :
Often they come to the door in a pleasant kind of a
    dream.
They come and sit by my chair, they hover about my
    bed—
I am not always certain if they be alive or dead.

XXII

And yet I know for a truth, there's none of them left
    alive;
For Harry went at sixty, your father at sixty-five :
And Willy, my eldest-born, at nigh threescore and ten ;
I knew them all as babies, and now they're elderly men.

XXIII

For mine is a time of peace, it is not often I grieve ;
I am oftener sitting at home in my father's farm at eve :
And the neighbours come and laugh and gossip, and
    so do I ;
I find myself often laughing at things that have long
    gone by.

XXIV

To be sure the preacher says, our sins should make
    us sad :
But mine is a time of peace, and there is Grace to be
    had ;
And God, not man, is the Judge of us all when life
    shall cease ;
And in this Book, little Annie, the message is one of
    Peace.

XXV

And age is a time of peace, so it be free from pain,
And happy has been my life ; but I would not live it
    again.

I seem to be tired a little, that's all, and long for
rest ;
Only at your age, Annie, I could have wept with the
best.

XXVI

So Willy has gone, my beauty, my eldest-born, my
flower ;
But how can I weep for Willy, he has but gone for
an hour,—
Gone for a minute, my son, from this room into the
next ;
I, too, shall go in a minute. What time have I to
be vext?

XXVII

And Willy's wife has written, she never was over-
wise.
Get me my glasses, Annie: thank God that I keep
my eyes.
There is but a trifle left you, when I shall have past
away.
But stay with the old woman now : you cannot have
long to stay.

VII

RIZPAH

17—

I

WAILING, wailing, wailing, the wind over land and
sea—
And Willy's voice in the wind, 'O mother, come out
to me.'
Why should he call me to-night, when he knows that
I cannot go?
For the downs are as bright as day, and the full moon
stares at the snow.

II

We should be seen, my dear; they would spy us out of the town.
The loud black nights for us, and the storm rushing over the down,
When I cannot see my own hand, but am led by the creak of the chain,
And grovel and grope for my son till I find myself drenched with the rain.

III

Anything fallen again? nay—what was there left to fall?
I have taken them home, I have number'd the bones, I have hidden them all.
What am I saying? and what are *you*? do you come as a spy?
Falls? what falls? who knows? As the tree falls so must it lie.

IV

Who let her in? how *long* has she been? you—what have you heard?
Why did you sit so quiet? you never have spoken a word.
O—to pray with me—yes—a lady—none of their spies—
But the night has crept into my heart, and begun to darken my eyes.

V

Ah—you, that have lived so soft, what should *you* know of the night,
The blast and the burning shame and the bitter frost and the fright?
I have done it, while you were asleep—you were only made for the day.
I have gather'd my baby together—and now you may go your way.

VI

Nay—for it's kind of you, Madam, to sit by an old dying wife.
But say nothing hard of my boy, I have only an hour of life.
I kiss'd my boy in the prison, before he went out to die.
'They dared me to do it,' he said, and he never has told me a lie.
I whipt him for robbing an orchard once when he was but a child—
'The farmer dared me to do it,' he said; he was always so wild—
And idle—and couldn't be idle—my Willy—he never could rest.
The King should have made him a soldier, he would have been one of his best.

VII

But he lived with a lot of wild mates, and they never would let him be good;
They swore that he dare not rob the mail, and he swore that he would;
And he took no life, but he took one purse, and when all was done
He flung it among his fellows—I'll none of it, said my son.

VIII

I came into court to the Judge and the lawyers. I told them my tale,
God's own truth—but they kill'd him, they kill'd him for robbing the mail.
They hang'd him in chains for a show—we had always borne a good name—
To be hang'd for a thief—and then put away—isn't that enough shame?
Dust to dust—low down—let us hide! but they set him so high

That all the ships of the world could stare at him,
    passing by.
God 'ill pardon the hell-black raven and horrible fowls
    of the air,
But not the black heart of the lawyer who kill'd him
    and hang'd him there.

IX

And the jailer forced me away. I had bid him my
    last goodbye;
They had fasten'd the door of his cell. 'O mother!'
    I heard him cry.
I couldn't get back tho' I tried, he had something
    further to say,
And now I never shall know it. The jailer forced me
    away.

X

Then since I couldn't but hear that cry of my boy
    that was dead,
They seized me and shut me up: they fasten'd me
    down on my bed.
'Mother, O mother!'—he call'd in the dark to me
    year after year—
They beat me for that, they beat me—you know that
    I couldn't but hear;
And then at the last they found I had grown so stupid
    and still
They let me abroad again—but the creatures had
    worked their will.

XI

Flesh of my flesh was gone, but bone of my bone was
    left—
I stole them all from the lawyers—and you, will you
    call it a theft?—
My baby, the bones that had suck'd me, the bones
    that had laughed and had cried—
Theirs? O no! they are mine—not theirs—they had
    moved in my side.

XII

Do you think I was scared by the bones? I kiss'd 'em,
   I buried 'em all—
I can't dig deep, I am old—in the night by the church-
   yard wall.
My Willy 'ill rise up whole when the trumpet of
   judgment 'ill sound,
But I charge you never to say that I laid him in holy
   ground.

XIII

They would scratch him up—they would hang him
   again on the cursed tree.
Sin? O yes—we are sinners, I know—let all that
   be,
And read me a Bible verse of the Lord's good will
   toward men—
'Full of compassion and mercy, the Lord'—let me
   hear it again;
'Full of compassion and mercy—long-suffering.' Yes,
   O yes!
For the lawyer is born but to murder—the Saviour
   lives but to bless.
He'll never put on the black cap except for the worst
   of the worst,
And the first may be last—I have heard it in church—
   and the last may be first.
Suffering—O long-suffering—yes, as the Lord must
   know,
Year after year in the mist and the wind and the
   shower and the snow.

XIV

Heard, have you? what? they have told you he never
   repented his sin.
How do they know it? are *they* his mother? are *you*
   of his kin?

Heard! have you ever heard, when the storm on the
  downs began,
The wind that 'ill wail like a child and the sea that
  'ill moan like a man?

XV

Election, Election and Reprobation—it's all very
  well.
But I go to-night to my boy, and I shall not find him
  in Hell.
For I cared so much for my boy that the Lord has
  look'd into my care,
And He means me I'm sure to be happy with Willy,
  I know not where.

XVI

And if *he* be lost—but to save *my* soul, that is all
  your desire:
Do you think that I care for *my* soul if my boy be
  gone to the fire?
I have been with God in the dark—go, go, you may
  leave me alone—
You never have borne a child—you are just as hard
  as a stone.

XVII

Madam, I beg your pardon! I think that you mean
  to be kind,
But I cannot hear what you say for my Willy's voice
  in the wind—
The snow and the sky so bright—he used but to call
  in the dark,
And he calls to me now from the church and not
  from the gibbet—for hark!
Nay—you can hear it yourself—it is coming—shaking
  the walls—
Willy—the moon's in a cloud——Goodnight. I am
  going. He calls.

VIII

THE VISION OF SIN

I

I HAD a vision when the night was late:
A youth came riding toward a palace-gate.
He rode a horse with wings, that would have flown,
But that his heavy rider kept him down.
And from the palace came a child of sin,
And took him by the curls, and led him in,
Where sat a company with heated eyes,
Expecting when a fountain should arise:
A sleepy light upon their brows and lips—
As when the sun, a crescent of eclipse,
Dreams over lake and lawn, and isles and capes—
Suffused them, sitting, lying, languid shapes,
By heaps of gourds, and skins of wine, and piles of grapes.

II

Then methought I heard a mellow sound,
Gathering up from all the lower ground;
Narrowing in to where they sat assembled
Low voluptuous music winding trembled,
Wov'n in circles: they that heard it sigh'd,
Panted hand-in-hand with faces pale,
Swung themselves, and in low tones replied;
Till the fountain spouted, showering wide
Sleet of diamond-drift and pearly hail;
Then the music touch'd the gates and died;
Rose again from where it seem'd to fail,
Storm'd in orbs of song, a growing gale;
Till thronging in and in, to where they waited,
As 'twere a hundred-throated nightingale,
The strong tempestuous treble throbb'd and palpitated;
Ran into its giddiest whirl of sound,
Caught the sparkles, and in circles,
Purple gauzes, golden hazes, liquid mazes,

Flung the torrent rainbow round:
Then they started from their places,
Moved with violence, changed in hue,
Caught each other with wild grimaces,
Half-invisible to the view,
Wheeling with precipitate paces
To the melody, till they flew,
Hair, and eyes, and limbs, and faces,
Twisted hard in fierce embraces,
Like to Furies, like to Graces,
Dash'd together in blinding dew:
Till, kill'd with some luxurious agony,
The nerve-dissolving melody
Flutter'd headlong from the sky.

III

And then I look'd up toward a mountain-tract,
That girt the region with high cliff and lawn:
I saw that every morning, far withdrawn
Beyond the darkness and the cataract,
God made Himself an awful rose of dawn,
Unheeded: and detaching, fold by fold,
From those still heights, and, slowly drawing near,
A vapour heavy, hueless, formless, cold,
Came floating on for many a month and year,
Unheeded: and I thought I would have spoken,
And warn'd that madman ere it grew too late:
But, as in dreams, I could not. Mine was broken,
When that cold vapour touch'd the palace gate,
And link'd again. I saw within my head
A gray and gap-tooth'd man as lean as death,
Who slowly rode across a wither'd heath,
And lighted at a ruin'd inn, and said:

IV

'Wrinkled ostler, grim and thin!
  Here is custom come your way;
Take my brute, and lead him in,
  Stuff his ribs with mouldy hay.

' Bitter barmaid, waning fast !
   See that sheets are on my bed ;
What ! the flower of life is past :
   It is long before you wed.

' Slip-shod waiter, lank and sour,
   At the Dragon on the heath !
Let us have a quiet hour,
   Let us hob-and-nob with Death.

' I am old, but let me drink ;
   Bring me spices, bring me wine ;
I remember, when I think,
   That my youth was half divine.

' Wine is good for shrivell'd lips,
   When a blanket wraps the day,
When the rotten woodland drips,
   And the leaf is stamp'd in clay.

' Sit thee down, and have no shame,
   Cheek by jowl, and knee by knee :
What care I for any name ?
   What for order or degree ?

' Let me screw thee up a peg :
   Let me loose thy tongue with wine :
Callest thou that thing a leg ?
   Which is thinnest ? thine or mine ?

' Thou shalt not be saved by works :
   Thou hast been a sinner too :
Ruin'd trunks on wither'd forks,
   Empty scarecrows, I and you !

' Fill the cup, and fill the can :
   Have a rouse before the morn :
Every moment dies a man,
   Every moment one is born.

' We are men of ruin'd blood ;
   Therefore comes it we are wise.
Fish are we that love the mud,
   Rising to no fancy-flies.

'Name and fame! to fly sublime
  Thro' the courts, the camps, the schools,
Is to be the ball of Time,
  Bandied by the hands of fools.

'Friendship!—to be two in one—
  Let the canting liar pack!
Well I know, when I am gone,
  How she mouths behind my back.

'Virtue!—to be good and just—
  Every heart, when sifted well,
Is a clot of warmer dust,
  Mix'd with cunning sparks of hell.

'O! we two as well can look
  Whited thought and cleanly life
As the priest, above his book
  Leering at his neighbour's wife.

'Fill the cup, and fill the can:
  Have a rouse before the morn:
Every moment dies a man,
  Every moment one is born.

'Drink, and let the parties rave:
  They are filled with idle spleen;
Rising, falling, like a wave,
  For they know not what they mean.

'He that roars for liberty
  Faster binds a tyrant's power;
And the tyrant's cruel glee
  Forces on the freer hour.

'Fill the can, and fill the cup:
  All the windy ways of men
Are but dust that rises up,
  And is lightly laid again.

'Greet her with applausive breath,
  Freedom, gaily doth she tread;
In her right a civic wreath,
  In her left a human head.

'No, I love not what is new;
   She is of an ancient house:
And I think we know the hue
   Of that cap upon her brows.

'Let her go! her thirst she slakes
   Where the bloody conduit runs,
Then her sweetest meal she makes
   On the first-born of her sons.

'Drink to lofty hopes that cool—
   Visions of a perfect State:
Drink we, last, the public fool,
   Frantic love and frantic hate.

'Chant me now some wicked stave,
   Till thy drooping courage rise,
And the glow-worm of the grave
   Glimmer in thy rheumy eyes.

'Fear not thou to loose thy tongue;
   Set thy hoary fancies free;
What is loathsome to the young
   Savours well to thee and me.

'Change, reverting to the years,
   When thy nerves could understand
What there is in loving tears,
   And the warmth of hand in hand.

'Tell me tales of thy first love—
   April hopes, the fools of chance;
Till the graves begin to move,
   And the dead begin to dance.

'Fill the can, and fill the cup:
   All the windy ways of men
Are but dust that rises up,
   And is lightly laid again.

'Trooping from their mouldy dens
   The chap-fallen circle spreads:
Welcome, fellow-citizens,
   Hollow hearts and empty heads!

'You are bones, and what of that?
    Every face, however full,
Padded round with flesh and fat,
    Is but modell'd on a skull.

'Death is king, and Vivat Rex!
    Tread a measure on the stones,
Madam—if I know your sex,
    From the fashion of your bones.

'No, I cannot praise the fire
    In your eye—nor yet your lip:
All the more do I admire
    Joints of cunning workmanship.

'Lo! God's likeness—the ground-plan—
    Neither modell'd, glazed, nor framed:
Buss me, thou rough sketch of man,
    Far too naked to be shamed!

'Drink to Fortune, drink to Chance,
    While we keep a little breath!
Drink to heavy Ignorance!
    Hob-and-nob with brother Death!

'Thou art mazed, the night is long,
    And the longer night is near:
What! I am not all as wrong
    As a bitter jest is dear.

'Youthful hopes, by scores, to all,
    When the locks are crisp and curl'd;
Unto me my maudlin gall
    And my mockeries of the world.

'Fill the cup, and fill the can:
    Mingle madness, mingle scorn!
Dregs of life, and lees of man:
    Yet we will not die forlorn.'

v

The voice grew faint: there came a further change:
Once more uprose the mystic mountain-range:

Below were men and horses pierced with worms,
And slowly quickening into lower forms;
By shards and scurf of salt, and scum of dross,
Old plash of rains, and refuse patch'd with moss.
Then some one spake: 'Behold! it was a crime
Of sense avenged by sense that wore with time.'
Another said: 'The crime of sense became
The crime of malice, and is equal blame.'
And one: 'He had not wholly quench'd his power;
A little grain of conscience made him sour.'
At last I heard a voice upon the slope
Cry to the summit, 'Is there any hope?'
To which an answer peal'd from that high land,
But in a tongue no man could understand;
And on the glimmering limit far withdrawn
God made Himself an awful rose of dawn.

IX

THE TWO VOICES

A STILL small voice spake unto me,
'Thou art so full of misery,
Were it not better not to be?'

Then to the still small voice I said;
'Let me not cast in endless shade
What is so wonderfully made.'

To which the voice did urge reply;
'To-day I saw the dragon-fly
Come from the wells where he did lie.

'An inner impulse rent the veil
Of his old husk: from head to tail
Came out clear plates of sapphire mail.

'He dried his wings: like gauze they grew;
Thro' crofts and pastures wet with dew
A living flash of light he flew.'

I said, 'When first the world began,
Young Nature thro' five cycles ran,
And in the sixth she moulded man.

'She gave him mind, the lordliest
Proportion, and, above the rest,
Dominion in the head and breast.'

Thereto the silent voice replied;
'Self-blinded are you by your pride:
Look up thro' night: the world is wide.

'This truth within thy mind rehearse,
That in a boundless universe
Is boundless better, boundless worse.

'Think you this mould of hopes and fears
Could find no statelier than his peers
In yonder hundred million spheres?'

It spake, moreover, in my mind:
'Tho' thou wert scatter'd to the wind,
Yet is there plenty of the kind.'

Then did my response clearer fall:
'No compound of this earthly ball
Is like another, all in all.'

To which he answer'd scoffingly;
'Good soul! suppose I grant it thee,
Who'll weep for thy deficiency?

'Or will one beam be less intense,
When thy peculiar difference
Is cancell'd in the world of sense?'

I would have said, 'Thou canst not know,'
But my full heart, that work'd below,
Rain'd thro' my sight its overflow.

Again the voice spake unto me:
'Thou art so steep'd in misery,
Surely 'twere better not to be.

'Thine anguish will not let thee sleep,
Nor any train of reason keep:
Thou canst not think, but thou wilt weep.'

I said, 'The years with change advance:
If I make dark my countenance,
I shut my life from happier chance.

'Some turn this sickness yet might take,
Ev'n yet.' But he: 'What drug can make
A wither'd palsy cease to shake?'

I wept, 'Tho' I should die, I know
That all about the thorn will blow
In tufts of rosy-tinted snow;

'And men, thro' novel spheres of thought
Still moving after truth long sought,
Will learn new things when I am not.'

'Yet,' said the secret voice, 'some time,
Sooner or later, will gray prime
Make thy grass hoar with early rime.

'Not less swift souls that yearn for light,
Rapt after heaven's starry flight,
Would sweep the tracts of day and night.

'Not less the bee would range her cells,
The furzy prickle fire the dells,
The foxglove cluster dappled bells.'

I said that 'all the years invent;
Each month is various to present
The world with some development.

'Were this not well, to bide mine hour,
Tho' watching from a ruin'd tower
How grows the day of human power?'

'The highest-mounted mind,' he said,
'Still sees the sacred morning spread
The silent summit overhead.

'Will thirty seasons render plain
Those lonely lights that still remain,
Just breaking over land and main?

'Or make that morn, from his cold crown
And crystal silence creeping down,
Flood with full daylight glebe and town?

'Forerun thy peers, thy time, and let
Thy feet, millenniums hence, be set
In midst of knowledge, dream'd not yet.

'Thou hast not gain'd a real height,
Nor art thou nearer to the light,
Because the scale is infinite.

''Twere better not to breathe or speak,
Than cry for strength, remaining weak,
And seem to find, but still to seek.

'Moreover, but to seem to find
Asks what thou lackest, thought resign'd,
A healthy frame, a quiet mind.'

I said, 'When I am gone away,
"He dared not tarry," men will say,
Doing dishonour to my clay.'

'This is more vile,' he made reply,
'To breathe and loathe, to live and sigh,
Than once from dread of pain to die.

'Sick art thou—a divided will
Still heaping on the fear of ill
The fear of men, a coward still.

'Do men love thee? Art thou so bound
To men, that how thy name may sound
Will vex thee lying underground?

'The memory of the wither'd leaf
In endless time is scarce more brief
Than of the garner'd Autumn-sheaf.

'Go, vexed Spirit, sleep in trust;
The right ear, that is fill'd with dust,
Hears little of the false or just.'

'Hard task, to pluck resolve,' I cried,
'From emptiness and the waste wide
Of that abyss, or scornful pride!

'Nay—rather yet that I could raise
One hope that warm'd me in the days
While still I yearn'd for human praise.

'When, wide in soul and bold of tongue,
Among the tents I paused and sung,
The distant battle flash'd and rung.

'I sung the joyful Pæan clear,
And, sitting, burnish'd without fear
The brand, the buckler, and the spear—

'Waiting to strive a happy strife,
To war with falsehood to the knife,
And not to lose the good of life—

'Some hidden principle to move,
To put together, part and prove,
And mete the bounds of hate and love—

'As far as might be, to carve out
Free space for every human doubt,
That the whole mind might orb about—

'To search thro' all I felt or saw,
The springs of life, the depths of awe,
And reach the law within the law:

'At least, not rotting like a weed,
But, having sown some generous seed,
Fruitful of further thought and deed,

'To pass, when Life her light withdraws,
Not void of righteous self-applause,
Nor in a merely selfish cause—

'In some good cause, not in mine own,
To perish, wept for, honour'd, known,
And like a warrior overthrown;

'Whose eyes are dim with glorious tears,
When, soil'd with noble dust, he hears
His country's war-song thrill his ears:

'Then dying of a mortal stroke,
What time the foeman's line is broke,
And all the war is roll'd in smoke.'

'Yea!' said the voice, 'thy dream was good,
While thou abodest in the bud.
It was the stirring of the blood.

'If Nature put not forth her power
About the opening of the flower,
Who is it that could live an hour?

'Then comes the check, the change, the fall,
Pain rises up, old pleasures pall.
There is one remedy for all.

'Yet hadst thou, thro' enduring pain,
Link'd month to month with such a chain
Of knitted purport, all were vain.

'Thou hadst not between death and birth
Dissolved the riddle of the earth.
So were thy labour little-worth.

'That men with knowledge merely play'd,
I told thee—hardly nigher made,
Tho' scaling slow from grade to grade;

'Much less this dreamer, deaf and blind,
Named man, may hope some truth to find,
That bears relation to the mind.

'For every worm beneath the moon
Draws different threads, and late and soon
Spins, toiling out his own cocoon.

'Cry, faint not: either Truth is born
Beyond the polar gleam forlorn,
Or in the gateways of the morn.

'Cry, faint not, climb: the summits slope
Beyond the furthest flights of hope,
Wrapt in dense cloud from base to cope.

'Sometimes a little corner shines,
As over rainy mist inclines
A gleaming crag with belts of pines.

'I will go forward, sayest thou,
I shall not fail to find her now.
Look up, the fold is on her brow.

'If straight thy track, or if oblique,
Thou know'st not.   Shadows thou dost strike,
Embracing cloud, Ixion-like;

'And owning but a little more
Than beasts, abidest lame and poor,
Calling thyself a little lower

'Than angels.   Cease to wail and brawl!
Why inch by inch to darkness crawl?
There is one remedy for all.'

'O dull, one-sided voice,' said I,
'Wilt thou make everything a lie,
To flatter me that I may die?

'I know that age to age succeeds,
Blowing a noise of tongues and deeds,
A dust of systems and of creeds.

'I cannot hide that some have striven,
Achieving calm, to whom was given
The joy that mixes man with Heaven:

'Who, rowing hard against the stream,
Saw distant gates of Eden gleam,
And did not dream it was a dream;

'But heard, by secret transport led,
Ev'n in the charnels of the dead,
The murmur of the fountain-head—

'Which did accomplish their desire,
Bore and forbore, and did not tire,
Like Stephen, an unquenched fire.

'He heeded not reviling tones,
Nor sold his heart to idle moans,
Tho' cursed and scorn'd, and bruised with stones:

'But looking upward, full of grace,
He pray'd, and from a happy place
God's glory smote him on the face.'

The sullen answer slid betwixt:
'Not that the grounds of hope were fix'd,
The elements were kindlier mix'd.'

I said, 'I toil beneath the curse,
But, knowing not the universe,
I fear to slide from bad to worse.

'And that, in seeking to undo
One riddle, and to find the true,
I knit a hundred others new:

'Or that this anguish fleeting hence,
Unmanacled from bonds of sense,
Be fix'd and froz'n to permanence:

'For I go, weak from suffering here:
Naked I go, and void of cheer:
What is it that I may not fear?'

'Consider well,' the voice replied,
'His face, that two hours since hath died;
Wilt thou find passion, pain or pride?

'Will he obey when one commands?
Or answer should one press his hands?
He answers not, nor understands.

'His palms are folded on his breast:
There is no other thing express'd
But long disquiet merged in rest.

'His lips are very mild and meek:
Tho' one should smite him on the cheek,
And on the mouth, he will not speak.

'His little daughter, whose sweet face
He kiss'd, taking his last embrace,
Becomes dishonour to her race—

'His sons grow up that bear his name,
Some grow to honour, some to shame,—
But he is chill to praise or blame.

'He will not hear the north-wind rave,
Nor, moaning, household shelter crave
From winter rains that beat his grave.

'High up the vapours fold and swim:
About him broods the twilight dim:
The place he knew forgetteth him.'

'If all be dark, vague voice,' I said,
'These things are wrapt in doubt and dread,
Nor canst thou show the dead are dead.

'The sap dries up: the plant declines.
A deeper tale my heart divines.
Know I not Death? the outward signs?

'I found him when my years were few;
A shadow on the graves I knew,
And darkness in the village yew.

'From grave to grave the shadow crept:
In her still place the morning wept:
Touch'd by his feet the daisy slept.

'The simple senses crown'd his head:
"Omega! thou art Lord," they said,
"We find no motion in the dead."

' Why, if man rot in dreamless ease,
Should that plain fact, as taught by these,
Not make him sure that he shall cease?

' Who forged that other influence,
That heat of inward evidence,
By which he doubts against the sense?

' He owns the fatal gift of eyes,
That read his spirit blindly wise,
Not simple as a thing that dies.

' Here sits he shaping wings to fly :
His heart forebodes a mystery :
He names the name Eternity.

' That type of Perfect in his mind
In Nature can he nowhere find.
He sows himself on every wind.

' He seems to hear a Heavenly Friend,
And thro' thick veils to apprehend
A labour working to an end.

' The end and the beginning vex
His reason : many things perplex,
With motions, checks, and counterchecks.

' He knows a baseness in his blood
At such strange war with something good,
He may not do the thing he would.

' Heaven opens inward, chasms yawn,
Vast images in glimmering dawn,
Half shown, are broken and withdrawn.

' Ah ! sure within him and without,
Could his dark wisdom find it out,
There must be answer to his doubt,

' But thou canst answer not again.
With thine own weapon art thou slain,
Or thou wilt answer but in vain.

'The doubt would rest, I dare not solve.
In the same circle we revolve.
Assurance only breeds resolve.'

As when a billow, blown against,
Falls back, the voice with which I fenced
A little ceased, but recommenced.

'Where wert thou when thy father play'd
In his free field, and pastime made,
A merry boy in sun and shade?

'A merry boy they call'd him then,
He sat upon the knees of men
In days that never come again.

'Before the little ducts began
To feed thy bones with lime, and ran
Their course, till thou wert also man:

'Who took a wife, who rear'd his race,
Whose wrinkles gather'd on his face,
Whose troubles number with his days:

'A life of nothings, nothing-worth,
From that first nothing ere his birth
To that last nothing under earth!'

'These words,' I said, 'are like the rest;
No certain clearness, but at best
A vague suspicion of the breast:

'But if I grant, thou mightst defend
The thesis which thy words intend—
That to begin implies to end;

'Yet how should I for certain hold,
Because my memory is so cold,
That I first was in human mould?

'I cannot make this matter plain,
But I would shoot, howe'er in vain,
A random arrow from the brain.

'It may be that no life is found,
Which only to one engine bound
Falls off, but cycles always round.

'As old mythologies relate,
Some draught of Lethe might await
The slipping thro' from state to state.

'As here we find in trances, men
Forget the dream that happens then,
Until they fall in trance again.

'So might we, if our state were such
As one before, remember much,
For those two likes might meet and touch.

'But, if I lapsed from nobler place,
Some legend of a fallen race
Alone might hint of my disgrace;

'Some vague emotion of delight
In gazing up an Alpine height,
Some yearning toward the lamps of night;

'Or if thro' lower lives I came—
Tho' all experience past became
Consolidate in mind and frame—

'I might forget my weaker lot;
For is not our first year forgot?
The haunts of memory echo not.

'And men, whose reason long was blind,
From cells of madness unconfined,
Oft lose whole years of darker mind.

'Much more, if first I floated free,
As naked essence, must I be
Incompetent of memory:

'For memory dealing but with time,
And he with matter, could she climb
Beyond her own material prime?

'Moreover, something is or seems,
That touches me with mystic gleams,
Like glimpses of forgotten dreams—

'Of something felt, like something here;
Of something done, I know not where;
Such as no language may declare.'

The still voice laugh'd. 'I talk,' said he,
'Not with thy dreams. Suffice it thee
Thy pain is a reality.'

'But thou,' said I, 'hast missed thy mark,
Who sought'st to wreck my mortal ark,
By making all the horizon dark.

'Why not set forth, if I should do
This rashness, that which might ensue
With this old soul in organs new?

'Whatever crazy sorrow saith,
No life that breathes with human breath
Has ever truly long'd for death.

''Tis life, whereof our nerves are scant,
Oh life, not death, for which we pant;
More life, and fuller, that I want.'

I ceased, and sat as one forlorn.
Then said the voice, in quiet scorn,
'Behold, it is the Sabbath morn.'

And I arose, and I released
The casement, and the light increased
With freshness in the dawning east.

Like soften'd airs that blowing steal,
When meres begin to uncongeal,
The sweet church bells began to peal.

On to God's house the people prest:
Passing the place where each must rest,
Each enter'd like a welcome guest.

One walk'd between his wife and child,
With measured footfall firm and mild,
And now and then he gravely smiled.

The prudent partner of his blood
Lean'd on him, faithful, gentle, good,
Wearing the rose of womanhood.

And in their double love secure,
The little maiden walk'd demure,
Pacing with downward eyelids pure.

These three made unity so sweet,
My frozen heart began to beat,
Remembering its ancient heat.

I blest them, and they wander'd on :
I spoke, but answer came there none :
The dull and bitter voice was gone.

A second voice was at mine ear,
A little whisper silver-clear,
A murmur, 'Be of better cheer.'

As from some blissful neighbourhood,
A notice faintly understood,
'I see the end, and know the good.'

A little hint to solace woe,
A hint, a whisper breathing low,
'I may not speak of what I know.'

Like an Æolian harp that wakes
No certain air, but overtakes
Far thought with music that it makes :

Such seem'd the whisper at my side :
'What is it thou knowest, sweet voice?' I cried.
'A hidden hope,' the voice replied :

So heavenly-toned, that in that hour
From out my sullen heart a power
Broke, like the rainbow from the shower,

To feel, altho' no tongue can prove,
That every cloud, that spreads above
And veileth love, itself is love.

And forth into the fields I went,
And Nature's living motion lent
The pulse of hope to discontent.

I wonder'd at the bounteous hours,
The slow result of winter showers:
You scarce could see the grass for flowers.

I wonder'd, while I paced along:
The woods were fill'd so full with song,
There seem'd no room for sense of wrong;

And all so variously wrought,
I marvell'd how the mind was brought
To anchor by one gloomy thought;

And wherefore rather I made choice
To commune with that barren voice,
Than him that said, 'Rejoice! Rejoice!'

X

WAGES

GLORY of warrior, glory of orator, glory of song,
   Paid with a voice flying by to be lost on an endless sea—
Glory of Virtue, to fight, to struggle, to right the wrong—
   Nay, but she aim'd not at glory, no lover of glory she:
Give her the glory of going on, and still to be.

The wages of sin is death: if the wages of Virtue be dust,
   Would she have heart to endure for the life of the worm and the fly?

She desires no isles of the blest, no quiet seats of
    the just,
  To rest in a golden grove, or to bask in a summer
    sky:
Give her the wages of going on, and not to die.

XI

THE SAILOR BOY

He rose at dawn and, fired with hope,
  Shot o'er the seething harbour-bar,
And reach'd the ship and caught the rope,
  And whistled to the morning star.

And while he whistled long and loud
  He heard a fierce mermaiden cry,
'O boy, tho' thou art young and proud,
  I see the place where thou wilt lie.

'The sands and yeasty surges mix
  In caves about the dreary bay,
And on thy ribs the limpet sticks,
  And in thy heart the scrawl shall play.'

'Fool,' he answer'd, 'death is sure
  To those that stay and those that roam,
But I will nevermore endure
  To sit with empty hands at home.

'My mother clings about my neck,
  My sisters crying, "Stay for shame;"
My father raves of death and wreck,
  They are all to blame, they are all to blame.

'God help me! save I take my part
  Of danger on the roaring sea,
A devil rises in my heart,
  Far worse than any death to me.'

XII

THE VOYAGE

I

We left behind the painted buoy
  That tosses at the harbour-mouth;
And madly danced our hearts with joy,
  As fast we fleeted to the South:
How fresh was every sight and sound
  On open main or winding shore!
We knew the merry world was round,
  And we might sail for evermore.

II

Warm broke the breeze against the brow,
  Dry sang the tackle, sang the sail:
The Lady's-head upon the prow
  Caught the shrill salt, and sheer'd the gale.
The seas swell'd to meet the keel,
  And swept behind; so quick the run,
We felt the good ship shake and reel,
  We seem'd to sail into the Sun!

III

How oft we saw the Sun retire,
  And burn the threshold of the night,
Fall from his Ocean-lane of fire,
  And sleep beneath his pillar'd light!
How oft the purple-skirted robe
  Of twilight slowly downward drawn,
As thro' the slumber of the globe
  Again we dash'd into the dawn!

IV

New stars all night above the brim
  Of waters lighten'd into view;
They climb'd as quickly, for the rim
  Changed every moment as we flew.

Far ran the naked moon across
   The houseless ocean's heaving field,
Or flying shone, the silver boss
   Of her own halo's dusky shield;

V

The peaky islet shifted shapes,
   High towns on hills were dimly seen,
We past long lines of Northern capes
   And dewy Northern meadows green.
We came to warmer waves, and deep
   Across the boundless east we drove,
Where those long swells of breaker sweep
   The nutmeg rocks and isles of clove.

VI

By peaks that flamed, or, all in shade,
   Gloom'd the low coast and quivering brine
With ashy rains, that spreading made
   Fantastic plume or sable pine;
By sands and steaming flats, and floods
   Of mighty mouth, we scudded fast,
And hills and scarlet-mingled woods
   Glow'd for a moment as we past.

VII

O hundred shores of happy climes,
   How swiftly stream'd ye by the bark!
At times the whole sea burn'd, at times
   With wakes of fire we tore the dark;
At times a carven craft would shoot
   From havens hid in fairy bowers,
With naked limbs and flowers and fruit,
   But we nor paused for fruit nor flowers.

VIII -

For one fair Vision ever fled
   Down the waste waters day and night,
And still we follow'd where she led,
   In hope to gain upon her flight.

Her face was evermore unseen,
  And fixt upon the far sea-line;
But each man murmur'd, 'O my Queen,
  I follow till I make thee mine.'

IX

And now we lost her, now she gleam'd
  Like Fancy made of golden air,
Now nearer to the prow she seem'd
  Like Virtue firm, like Knowledge fair,
Now high on waves that idly burst
  Like Heavenly Hope she crown'd the sea,
And now, the bloodless point reversed,
  She bore the blade of Liberty.

X

And only one among us—him
  We pleased not—he was seldom pleased:
He saw not far: his eyes were dim:
  But ours he swore were all diseased.
'A ship of fools,' he shriek'd in spite,
  'A ship of fools,' he sneer'd and wept.
And overboard one stormy night
  He cast his body, and on we swept.

XI

And never sail of ours was furl'd,
  Nor anchor dropt at eve or morn;
We lov'd the glories of the world,
  But laws of nature were our scorn.
For blasts would rise and rave and cease,
  But whence were those that drove the sail
Across the whirlwind's heart of peace,
  And to and thro' the counter gale?

XII

Again to colder climes we came,
  For still we follow'd where she led:
Now mate is blind and captain lame,
  And half the crew are sick or dead,

But, blind or lame or sick or sound,
  We follow that which flies before :
We know the merry world is round,
  And we may sail for evermore.

XIII

THE DAY-DREAM

PROLOGUE

O LADY FLORA, let me speak :
  A pleasant hour has passed away
While, dreaming on your damask cheek,
  The dewy sister-eyelids lay.
As by the lattice you reclined,
  I went thro' many wayward moods
To see you dreaming—and, behind,
  A summer crisp with shining woods.
And I too dream'd, until at last
  Across my fancy, brooding warm,
The reflex of a legend past,
  And loosely settled into form.
And would you have the thought I had,
  And see the vision that I saw,
Then take the broidery-frame, and add
  A crimson to the quaint Macaw,
And I will tell it. Turn your face,
  Nor look with that too-earnest eye—
The rhymes are dazzled from their place,
  And order'd words asunder fly.

THE SLEEPING PALACE

I

THE varying year with blade and sheaf
  Clothes and reclothes the happy plains,
Here rests the sap within the leaf,
  Here stays the blood along the veins.

Faint shadows, vapours lightly curl'd,
    Faint murmurs from the meadows come,
Like hints and echoes of the world
    To spirits folded in the womb.

II

Soft lustre bathes the range of urns
    On every slanting terrace-lawn.
The fountain to his place returns
    Deep in the garden lake withdrawn.
Here droops the banner on the tower,
    On the hall-hearths the festal fires,
The peacock in his laurel bower,
    The parrot in his gilded wires.

III

Roof-haunting martins warm their eggs:
    In these, in those the life is stay'd.
The mantles from the golden pegs
    Droop sleepily: no sound is made,
Not even of a gnat that sings.
    More like a picture seemeth all
Than those old portraits of old kings,
    That watch the sleepers from the wall.

IV

Here sits the Butler with a flask
    Between his knees, half-drain'd; and there
The wrinkled steward at his task,
    The maid-of-honour blooming fair;
The page has caught her hand in his:
    Her lips are sever'd as to speak:
His own are pouted to a kiss:
    The blush is fix'd upon her cheek.

V

Till all the hundred summers pass,
    The beams, that thro' the Oriel shine,
Make prisms in every carven glass,
    And beaker brimm'd with noble wine.

Each baron at the banquet sleeps,
    Grave faces gather'd in a ring.
His state the king reposing keeps.
    He must have been a jovial king.

VI

All round a hedge upshoots, and shows
    At distance like a little wood;
Thorns, ivies, woodbine, mistletoes,
    And grapes with bunches red as blood;
All creeping plants, a wall of green
    Close-matted, bur and brake and briar,
And glimpsing over these, just seen,
    High up, the topmost palace spire.

VII

When will the hundred summers die,
    And thought and time be born again,
And newer knowledge, drawing nigh,
    Bring truth that sways the soul of men?
Here all things in their place remain,
    As all were order'd, ages since.
Come, Care and Pleasure, Hope and Pain,
    And bring the fated fairy Prince.

THE SLEEPING BEAUTY

I

YEAR after year unto her feet,
    She lying on her couch alone,
Across the purple coverlet,
    The maiden's jet-black hair has grown,
On either side her tranced form
    Forth streaming from a braid of pearl:
The slumbrous light is rich and warm,
    And moves not on the rounded curl.

II

The silk star-broider'd coverlid
   Unto her limbs itself doth mould
Languidly ever ; and, amid
   Her full black ringlets downward roll'd,
Glows forth each softly-shadow'd arm
   With bracelets of the diamond bright :
Her constant beauty doth inform
   Stillness with love, and day with light.

III

She sleeps : her breathings are not heard
   In palace chambers far apart.
The fragrant tresses are not stirr'd
   That lie upon her charmed heart.
She sleeps : on either hand upswells
   The gold-fringed pillow lightly prest :
She sleeps, nor dreams, but ever dwells
   A perfect form in perfect rest.

THE ARRIVAL

I

ALL precious things, discover'd late,
   To those that seek them issue forth ;
For love in sequel works with fate,
   And draws the veil from hidden worth.
He travels far from other skies—
   His mantle glitters on the rocks—
A fairy Prince, with joyful eyes,
   And lighter-footed than the fox.

II

The bodies and the bones of those
   That strove in other days to pass,
Are wither'd in the thorny close,
   Or scatter'd blanching on the grass.
He gazes on the silent dead :
   ' They perish'd in their daring deeds.'
This proverb flashes thro' his head,
   ' The many fail : the one succeeds.'

III

He comes, scarce knowing what he seeks:
  He breaks the hedge: he enters there:
The colour flies into his cheeks:
  He trusts to light on something fair;
For all his life the charm did talk
  About his path, and hover near
With words of promise in his walk,
  And whisper'd voices at his ear.

IV

More close and close his footsteps wind:
  The Magic Music in his heart
Beats quick and quicker, till he find
  The quiet chamber far apart.
His spirit flutters like a lark,
  He stoops—to kiss her—on his knee.
'Love, if thy tresses be so dark,
  How dark those hidden eyes must be!

THE REVIVAL

I

A TOUCH, a kiss! the charm was snapt.
  There rose a noise of striking clocks,
And feet that ran, and doors that clapt,
  And barking dogs, and crowing cocks;
A fuller light illumined all,
  A breeze thro' all the garden swept,
A sudden hubbub shook the hall,
  And sixty feet the fountain leapt.

II

The hedge broke in, the banner blew,
  The butler drank, the steward scrawl'd,
The fire shot up, the martin flew,
  The parrot scream'd, the peacock squall'd,
The maid and page renew'd their strife,
  The palace bang'd, and buzz'd and clackt
And all the long-pent stream of life
  Dash'd downward in a cataract.

III

And last with these the king awoke,
    And in his chair himself uprear'd,
And yawn'd, and rubb'd his face, and spoke,
    'By holy rood, a royal beard!
How say you? we have slept, my lords.
    My beard has grown into my lap.'
The barons swore, with many words,
    'Twas but an after-dinner's nap.

IV

'Pardy,' return'd the king, 'but still
    My joints are somewhat stiff or so.
My lord, and shall we pass the bill
    I mention'd half an hour ago?'
The chancellor, sedate and vain,
    In courteous words return'd reply:
But dallied with his golden chain,
    And, smiling, put the question by.

THE DEPARTURE

I

AND on her lover's arm she leant,
    And round her waist she felt it fold,
And far across the hills they went
    In that new world which is the old:
Across the hills, and far away
    Beyond their utmost purple rim,
And deep into the dying day
    The happy princess follow'd him.

II

'I'd sleep another hundred years,
    O love, for such another kiss;'
'O wake for ever, love,' she hears,
    'O love, 'twas such as this and this.'
And o'er them many a sliding star,
    And many a merry wind was borne,
And, stream'd thro' many a golden bar,
    The twilight melted into morn.

III

'O eyes long laid in happy sleep!'
  'O happy sleep, that lightly fled!'
'O happy kiss, that woke thy sleep!'
  'O love, thy kiss would wake the dead!'
And o'er them many a flowing range
  Of vapour buoy'd the crescent-bark,
And, rapt thro' many a rosy change,
  The twilight died into the dark.

IV

'A hundred summers! can it be?
  And whither goest thou, tell me where?'
'O seek my father's court with me,
  For there are greater wonders there.'
And o'er the hills, and far away
  Beyond their utmost purple rim,
Beyond the night, across the day,
  Thro' all the world she follow'd him.

MORAL

I

So, Lady Flora, take my lay,
  And if you find no moral there,
Go, look in any glass and say,
  What moral is in being fair.
Oh, to what uses shall we put
  The wildweed-flower that simply blows?
And is there any moral shut
  Within the bosom of the rose?

II

But any man that walks the mead,
  In bud or blade, or bloom, may find,
According as his humours lead,
  A meaning suited to his mind.
And liberal applications lie
  In Art like Nature, dearest friend;
So 'twere to cramp its use, if I
  Should hook it to some useful end.

L'ENVOI

I

You shake your head. A random string
    Your finer female sense offends.
Well—were it not a pleasant thing
    To fall asleep with all one's friends;
To pass with all our social ties
    To silence from the paths of men;
And every hundred years to rise
    And learn the world, and sleep again;
To sleep thro' terms of mighty wars,
    And wake on science grown to more,
On secrets of the brain, the stars,
    As wild as aught of fairy lore;
And all that else the years will show,
    The Poet-forms of stronger hours,
The vast Republics that may grow,
    The Federations and the Powers;
Titanic forces taking birth
    In divers seasons, divers climes;
For we are Ancients of the earth,
    And in the morning of the times.

II

So sleeping, so aroused from sleep
    Thro' sunny decads new and strange,
Or gay quinquenniads would we reap
    The flower and quintessence of change.

III

Ah, yet would I—and would I might!
    So much your eyes my fancy take—
Be still the first to leap to light
    That I might kiss those eyes awake!
For, am I right, or am I wrong,
    To choose your own you did not care;
You'd have *my* moral from the song,
    And I will take my pleasure there:

And, am I right or am I wrong,
  My fancy, ranging thro' and thro',
To search a meaning for the song,
  Perforce will still revert to you;
Nor finds a closer truth than this
  All-graceful head, so richly curl'd,
And evermore a costly kiss
  The prelude to some brighter world.

IV

For since the time when Adam first
  Embraced his Eve in happy hour,
And every bird of Eden burst
  In carol, every bud to flower,
What eyes, like thine, have waken'd hopes,
  What lips, like thine, so sweetly join'd?
Where on the double rosebud droops
  The fulness of the pensive mind;
Which all too dearly self-involved,
  Yet sleeps a dreamless sleep to me;
A sleep by kisses undissolved,
  That lets thee neither hear nor see:
But break it. In the name of wife,
  And in the rights that name may give,
Are clasp'd the moral of thy life,
  And that for which I care to live.

EPILOGUE

So, Lady Flora, take my lay,
  And, if you find a meaning there,
O whisper to your glass, and say,
  'What wonder, if he thinks me fair?'
What wonder I was all unwise,
  To shape the song for your delight
Like long-tail'd birds of Paradise
  That float thro' Heaven, and cannot light?
Or old-world trains, upheld at court
  By Cupid-boys of blooming hue—
But take it—earnest wed with sport,
  And either sacred unto you.

XIV

THE SEA-FAIRIES

SLOW sail'd the weary mariners and saw,
Betwixt the green brink and the running foam,
Sweet faces, rounded arms, and bosoms prest
To little harps of gold; and while they mused
Whispering to each other half in fear,
Shrill music reach'd them on the middle sea.

Whither away, whither away, whither away? fly no
    more. .
Whither away from the high green field, and the happy
    blossoming shore?
Day and night to the billow the fountain calls:
Down shower the gambolling waterfalls
From wandering over the lea:
Out of the live-green heart of the dells
They freshen the silvery-crimson shells,
And thick with white bells the clover-hill swells
High over the full-toned sea:
O hither, come hither and furl your sails,
Come hither to me and to me:
Hither, come hither and frolic and play;
Here it is only the mew that wails;
We will sing to you all the day:
Mariner, mariner, furl your sails,
For here are the blissful downs and dales,
And merrily, merrily carol the gales,
And the spangle dances in bight and bay,
And the rainbow forms and flies on the land
Over the islands free;
And the rainbow lives in the curve of the sand;
Hither, come hither and see;
And the rainbow hangs on the poising wave,
And sweet is the colour of cove and cave,
And sweet shall your welcome be:
O hither, come hither, and be our lords,
For merry brides are we:

We will kiss sweet kisses, and speak sweet words:
O listen, listen, your eyes shall glisten
With pleasure and love and jubilee:
O listen, listen, your eyes shall glisten
When the sharp clear twang of the golden chords
Runs up the ridged sea.
Who can light on as happy a shore
All the world o'er, all the world o'er?
Whither away? listen and stay: mariner, mariner, fly
    no more.

XV

THE LOTOS-EATERS

'Courage!' he said, and pointed toward the land,
'This mounting wave will roll us shoreward soon.'
In the afternoon they came unto a land
In which it seemed always afternoon.
All round the coast the languid air did swoon,
Breathing like one that hath a weary dream.
Full-faced above the valley stood the moon;
And like a downward smoke, the slender stream
Along the cliff to fall and pause and fall did seem.

A land of streams! some, like a downward smoke,
Slow-dropping veils of thinnest lawn, did go;
And some thro' wavering lights and shadows broke,
Rolling a slumbrous sheet of foam below.
They saw the gleaming river seaward flow
From the inner land: far off, three mountain-tops,
Three silent pinnacles of aged snow,
Stood sunset-flush'd: and, dew'd with showery
    drops,
Up-clomb the shadowy pine above the woven copse.

The charmed sunset linger'd low adown
In the red West: thro' mountain clefts the dale
Was seen far inland, and the yellow down
Border'd with palm, and many a winding vale
And meadow, set with slender galingale;

A land where all things always seem'd the same!
And round about the keel with faces pale,
Dark faces pale against that rosy flame,
The mild-eyed melancholy Lotos-eaters came.

Branches they bore of that enchanted stem,
Laden with flower and fruit, whereof they gave
To each, but whoso did receive of them,
And taste, to him the gushing of the wave
Far far away did seem to mourn and rave
On alien shores; and if his fellow spake,
His voice was thin, as voices from the grave;
And deep-asleep he seem'd, yet all awake,
And music in his ears his beating heart did make.

They sat them down upon the yellow sand,
Between the sun and moon upon the shore;
And sweet it was to dream of Fatherland,
Of child, and wife, and slave; but evermore
Most weary seem'd the sea, weary the oar,
Weary the wandering fields of barren foam.
Then some one said, 'We will return no more;'
And all at once they sang, 'Our island home
Is far beyond the wave; we will no longer roam.'

CHORIC SONG

I

THERE is sweet music here that softer falls
Than petals from blown roses on the grass,
Or night-dews on still waters between walls
Of shadowy granite, in a gleaming pass;
Music that gentlier on the spirit lies,
Than tir'd eyelids upon tir'd eyes;
Music that brings sweet sleep down from the blissful
    skies.
Here are cool mosses deep,
And thro' the moss the ivies creep,
And in the stream the long-leaved flowers weep,
    And from the craggy ledge the poppy hangs in
    sleep.

II

Why are we weigh'd upon with heaviness,
And utterly consumed with sharp distress,
While all things else have rest from weariness?
All things have rest: why should we toil alone,
We only toil, who are the first of things,
And make perpetual moan,
Still from one sorrow to another thrown:
Nor ever fold our wings,
And cease from wanderings,
Nor steep our brows in slumber's holy balm;
Nor harken what the inner spirit sings,
'There is no joy but calm!'
Why should we only toil, the roof and crown of things?

III

Lo! in the middle of the wood,
The folded leaf is woo'd from out the bud
With winds upon the branch, and there
Grows green and broad, and takes no care,
Sun-steep'd at noon, and in the moon
Nightly dew-fed; and turning yellow
Falls, and floats adown the air.
Lo! sweeten'd with the summer light,
The full-juiced apple, waxing over-mellow,
Drops in a silent autumn night.
All its allotted length of days,
The flower ripens in its place,
Ripens and fades, and falls, and hath no toil,
Fast-rooted in the fruitful soil.

IV

Hateful is the dark-blue sky,
Vaulted o'er the dark-blue sea.
Death is the end of life; ah, why
Should life all labour be?
Let us alone. Time driveth onward fast,
And in a little while our lips are dumb.
Let us alone. What is it that will last?

All things are taken from us, and become
Portions and parcels of the dreadful Past.
Let us alone. What pleasure can we have
To war with evil? Is there any peace
In ever climbing up the climbing wave?
All things have rest, and ripen toward the grave
In silence; ripen, fall and cease:
Give us long rest or death, dark death, or dreamful ease.

V

How sweet it were, hearing the downward stream,
With half-shut eyes ever to seem
Falling asleep in a half-dream!
To dream and dream, like yonder amber light,
Which will not leave the myrrh-bush on the height;
To hear each other's whisper'd speech;
Eating the Lotos day by day,
To watch the crisping ripples on the beach,
And tender curving lines of creamy spray;
To lend our hearts and spirits wholly
To the influence of mild-minded melancholy;
To muse and brood and live again in memory,
With those old faces of our infancy
Heap'd over with a mound of grass,
Two handfuls of white dust, shut in an urn of brass!

VI

Dear is the memory of our wedded lives,
And dear the last embraces of our wives
And their warm tears: but all hath suffer'd change:
For surely now our household hearths are cold:
Our sons inherit us: our looks are strange:
And we should come like ghosts to trouble joy.
Or else the island princes over-bold
Have eat our substance, and the minstrel sings
Before them of the ten years' war in Troy,
And our great deeds, as half-forgotten things.
Is there confusion in the little isle?
Let what is broken so remain.
The Gods are hard to reconcile:

'Tis hard to settle order once again.
There *is* confusion worse than death,
Trouble on trouble, pain on pain,
Long labour unto aged breath,
Sore task to hearts worn out by many wars
And eyes grown dim with gazing on the pilot-stars.

VII

But, propt on beds of amaranth and moly,
How sweet (while warm airs lull us, blowing lowly)
With half-dropt eyelid still,
Beneath a heaven dark and holy,
To watch the long bright river drawing slowly
His waters from the purple hill—
To hear the dewy echoes calling
From cave to cave thro' the thick-twined vine—
To watch the emerald-colour'd water falling
Thro' many a wov'n acanthus-wreath divine!
Only to hear and see the far-off sparkling brine,
Only to hear were sweet, stretch'd out beneath the pine.

VIII

The Lotos blooms below the barren peak:
The Lotos blows by every winding creek:
All day the wind breathes low with mellower tone:
Thro' every hollow cave and alley lone
Round and round the spicy downs the yellow Lotos-dust is blown.
We have had enough of action, and of motion we,
Roll'd to starboard, roll'd to larboard, when the surge was seething free,
Where the wallowing monster spouted his foam-fountains in the sea.
Let us swear an oath, and keep it with an equal mind,
In the hollow Lotos-land to live and lie reclined
On the hills like Gods together, careless of mankind.
For they lie beside their nectar, and the bolts are hurl'd
Far below them in the valleys, and the clouds are lightly curl'd

Round their golden houses, girdled with the gleaming world:
Where they smile in secret, looking over wasted lands,
Blight and famine, plague and earthquake, roaring deeps and fiery sands,
Clanging fights, and flaming towns, and sinking ships, and praying hands.
But they smile, they find a music centred in a doleful song
Steaming up, a lamentation and an ancient tale of wrong,
Like a tale of little meaning tho' the words are strong;
Chanted from an ill-used race of men that cleave the soil,
Sow the seed, and reap the harvest with enduring toil,
Storing yearly little dues of wheat, and wine and oil;
Till they perish and they suffer—some, 'tis whisper'd—down in hell
Suffer endless anguish, others in Elysian valleys dwell,
Resting weary limbs at last on beds of asphodel.
Surely, surely, slumber is more sweet than toil, the shore
Than labour in the deep mid-ocean, wind and wave and oar;
Oh rest ye, brother mariners, we will not wander more.

XVI

THE VOYAGE OF MAELDUNE

(FOUNDED ON AN IRISH LEGEND. A.D. 700)

I

I WAS the chief of the race—he had stricken my father dead—
But I gather'd my fellows together, I swore I would strike off his head.
Each of them look'd like a king, and was noble in birth as in worth,
And each of them boasted he sprang from the oldest race upon earth.

Each was as brave in the fight as the bravest hero of
    song,
And each of them liefer had died than have done one
    another a wrong.
He lived on an isle in the ocean—we sail'd on a
    Friday morn—
He that had slain my father the day before I was
    born.

II

And we came to the isle in the ocean, and there on
    the shore was he.
But a sudden blast blew us out and away thro' a
    boundless sea.

III

And we came to the Silent Isle that we never had
    touch'd at before,
Where a silent ocean always broke on a silent shore,
And the brooks glitter'd on in the light without sound,
    and the long waterfalls
Pour'd in a thunderless plunge to the base of the
    mountain walls,
And the poplar and cypress unshaken by storm
    flourish'd up beyond sight,
And the pine shot aloft from the crag to an unbeliev-
    able height,
And high in the heaven above it there flicker'd a
    songless lark,
And the cock couldn't crow, and the bull couldn't low,
    and the dog couldn't bark.
And round it we went, and thro' it, but never a mur-
    mur, a breath—
It was all of it fair as life, it was all of it quiet as
    death,
And we hated the beautiful Isle, for whenever we
    strove to speak
Our voices were thinner and fainter than any flitter-
    mouse-shriek;
And the men that were mighty of tongue and could
    raise such a battle-cry

That a hundred who heard it would rush on a thousand lances and die—
O they to be dumb'd by the charm!—so fluster'd with anger were they
They almost fell on each other; but after we sail'd away.

IV

And we came to the Isle of Shouting, we landed, a score of wild birds
Cried from the topmost summit with human voices and words;
Once in an hour they cried, and whenever their voices peal'd
The steer fell down at the plow and the harvest died from the field,
And the men dropt dead in the valleys and half of the cattle went lame,
And the roof sank in on the hearth, and the dwelling broke into flame;
And the shouting of these wild birds ran into the hearts of my crew,
Till they shouted along with the shouting and seized one another and slew;
But I drew them the one from the other; I saw that we could not stay,
And we left the dead to the birds and we sail'd with our wounded away.

V

And we came to the Isle of Flowers: their breath met us out on the seas,
For the Spring and the middle Summer sat each on the lap of the breeze;
And the red passion-flower to the cliffs, and the dark-blue clematis, clung,
And starr'd with a myriad blossom the long convolvulus hung;
And the topmost spire of the mountain was lilies in lieu of snow,
And the lilies like glaciers winded down, running out below

Thro' the fire of the tulip and poppy, the blaze of gorse, and the blush
Of millions of roses that sprang without leaf or a thorn from the bush;
And the whole isle-side flashing down from the peak without ever a tree
Swept like a torrent of gems from the sky to the blue of the sea;
And we roll'd upon capes of crocus and vaunted our kith and our kin,
And we wallow'd in beds of lilies, and chanted the triumph of Finn,
Till each like a golden image was pollen'd from head to feet
And each was as dry as a cricket, with thirst in the middle-day heat.
Blossom and blossom, and promise of blossom, but never a fruit!
And we hated the Flowering Isle, as we hated the isle that was mute,
And we tore up the flowers by the million and flung them in bight and bay,
And we left but a naked rock, and in anger we sail'd away.

VI

And we came to the Isle of Fruits: all round from the cliffs and the capes,
Purple or amber, dangled a hundred fathom of grapes,
And the warm melon lay like a little sun on the tawny sand,
And the fig ran up from the beach and rioted over the land,
And the mountain arose like a jewell'd throne thro' the fragrant air,
Glowing with all-colour'd plums and with golden masses of pear,
And the crimson and scarlet of berries that flamed upon bine and vine,
But in every berry and fruit was the poisonous pleasure of wine;

And the peak of the mountain was apples, the hugest that ever were seen,
And they prest, as they grew, on each other, with hardly a leaflet between,
And all of them redder than rosiest health or than utterest shame,
And setting, when Even descended, the very sunset aflame;
And we stay'd three days, and we gorged and we madden'd, till every one drew
His sword on his fellow to slay him, and ever they struck and they slew;
And myself, I had eaten but sparely, and fought till I sunder'd the fray,
Then I bad them remember my father's death, and we sail'd away.

VII

And we came to the Isle of Fire: we were lured by the light from afar,
For the peak sent up one league of fire to the Northern Star;
Lured by the glare and the blare, but scarcely could stand upright,
For the whole isle shudder'd and shook like a man in a mortal affright;
We were giddy besides with the fruits we had gorged, and so crazed that at last
There were some leap'd into the fire; and away we sail'd, and we past
Over that undersea isle, where the water is clearer than air:
Down we look'd: what a garden! O bliss, what a Paradise there!
Towers of a happier time, low down in a rainbow deep
Silent palaces, quiet fields of eternal sleep!
And three of the gentlest and best of my people, whate'er I could say,
Plunged head down in the sea, and the Paradise trembled away.

VIII

And we came to the Bounteous Isle, where the heavens lean low on the land,
And ever at dawn from the cloud glitter'd o'er us a sunbright hand,
Then it open'd and dropt at the side of each man, as he rose from his rest,
Bread enough for his need till the labourless day dipt under the West;
And we wander'd about it and thro' it. O never was time so good!
And we sang of the triumphs of Finn, and the boast of our ancient blood,
And we gazed at the wandering wave as we sat by the gurgle of springs,
And we chanted the songs of the Bards and the glories of fairy kings;
But at length we began to be weary, to sigh, and to stretch and yawn,
Till we hated the Bounteous Isle and the sunbright hand of the dawn,
For there was not an enemy near, but the whole green Isle was our own,
And we took to playing at ball, and we took to throwing the stone,
And we took to playing at battle, but that was a perilous play,
For the passion of battle was in us, we slew and we sail'd away.

IX

And we came to the Isle of Witches and heard their musical cry—
'Come to us, O come, come' in the stormy red of a sky
Dashing the fires and the shadows of dawn on the beautiful shapes,
For a wild witch naked as heaven stood on each of the loftiest capes,

And a hundred ranged on the rock like white sea-
    birds in a row,
And a hundred gamboll'd and pranced on the wrecks
    in the sand below,
And a hundred splash'd from the ledges, and bosom'd
    the burst of the spray,
But I knew we should fall on each other, and hastily
    sail'd away.

X

And we came in an evil time to the Isle of the Double
    Towers,
One was of smooth-cut stone, one carved all over with
    flowers,
But an earthquake always moved in the hollows under
    the dells,
And they shock'd on each other and butted each other
    with clashing of bells,
And the daws flew out of the Towers and jangled and
    wrangled in vain,
And the clash and boom of the bells rang into the
    heart and the brain,
Till the passion of battle was on us, and all took sides
    with the Towers,
There were some for the clean-cut stone, there were
    more for the carven flowers,
And the wrathful thunder of God peal'd over us all the
    day,
For the one half slew the other, and after we sail'd
    away.

XI

And we came to the Isle of a Saint who had sail'd
    with St. Brendan of yore,
He had lived ever since on the Isle and his winters
    were fifteen score,
And his voice was low as from other worlds, and his
    eyes were sweet,
And his white hair sank to his heels and his white
    beard fell to his feet,

And he spake to me, 'O Maeldune, let be this purpose of thine !
Remember the words of the Lord when he told us "Vengeance is mine !"
His fathers have slain thy fathers in war or in single strife,
Thy fathers have slain his fathers, each taken a life for a life,
Thy father had slain his father, how long shall the murder last ?
Go back to the Isle of Finn and suffer the Past to be Past.'
And we kiss'd the fringe of his beard and we pray'd as we heard him pray,
And the Holy man he assoil'd us, and sadly we sail'd away.

XII

And we came to the Isle we were blown from, and there on the shore was he,
The man that had slain my father. I saw him and let him be.
O weary was I of the travel, the trouble, the strife and the sin,
When I landed again, with a tithe of my men, on the Isle of Finn.

XVII

THE DYING SWAN

I

The plain was grassy, wild and bare,
Wide, wild, and open to the air,
Which had built up everywhere
   An under-roof of doleful gray.
With an inner voice the river ran,
Adown it floated a dying swan,

And loudly did lament.
It was the middle of the day.
Ever the weary wind went on,
   And took the reed-tops as it went.

II

Some blue peaks in the distance rose,
And white against the cold-white sky,
Shone out their crowning snows.
   One willow over the river wept,
And shook the wave as the wind did sigh;
Above in the wind was the swallow,
     Chasing itself at its own wild will,
     And far thro' the marish green and still
     The tangled water-courses slept,
Shot over with purple, and green, and yellow.

III

The wild swan's death-hymn took the soul
Of that waste place with joy
Hidden in sorrow: at first to the ear
The warble was low, and full and clear;
And floating about the under-sky,
Prevailing in weakness, the coronach stole
Sometimes afar, and sometimes anear;
But anon her awful jubilant voice,
With a music strange and manifold,
Flow'd forth on a carol free and bold;
As when a mighty people rejoice
With shawms, and with cymbals, and harps of gold,
And the tumult of their acclaim is roll'd
Thro' the open gates of the city afar,
To the shepherd who watcheth the evening star.
And the creeping mosses and clambering weeds,
And the willow-branches hoar and dank,
And the wavy swell of the soughing reeds,
And the wave-worn horns of the echoing bank,
And the silvery marish-flowers that throng
The desolate creeks and pools among,
Were flooded over with eddying song.

XVIII

The splendour falls on castle walls
    And snowy summits old in story:
The long light shakes across the lakes,
    And the wild cataract leaps in glory.
Blow, bugle, blow, set the wild echoes flying,
Blow, bugle; answer, echoes, dying, dying, dying.

    O hark, O hear! how thin and clear,
        And thinner, clearer, farther going!
    O sweet and far from cliff and scar
        The horns of Elfland faintly blowing!
Blow, let us hear the purple glens replying:
Blow, bugle; answer, echoes, dying, dying, dying.

    O love, they die in yon rich sky,
        They faint on hill or field or river:
    Our echoes roll from soul to soul,
        And grow for ever and for ever.
Blow, bugle, blow, set the wild echoes flying,
And answer, echoes, answer, dying, dying, dying.

XIX

THE BROOK

I come from haunts of coot and hern,
    I make a sudden sally,
And sparkle out among the fern,
    To bicker down a valley.

By thirty hills I hurry down,
    Or slip between the ridges,
By twenty thorps, a little town,
    And half a hundred bridges.

Till last by Philip's farm I flow
    To join the brimming river,
For men may come and men may go,
    But I go on for ever.

The Brook

I CHATTER over stony ways,
   In little sharps and trebles,
I bubble into eddying bays,
   I babble on the pebbles.

With many a curve my banks I fret
   By many a field and fallow,
And many a fairy foreland set
   With willow-weed and mallow.

I chatter, chatter, as I flow
   To join the brimming river,
For men may come and men may go,
   But I go on for ever.

I WIND about, and in and out,
   With here a blossom sailing,
And here and there a lusty trout,
   And here and there a grayling,

And here and there a foamy flake
   Upon me, as I travel
With many a silvery waterbreak
   Above the golden gravel,

And draw them all along, and flow
   To join the brimming river,
For men may come and men may go,
   But I go on for ever.

I STEAL by lawns and grassy plots,
   I slide by hazel covers;
I move the sweet forget-me-nots
   That grow for happy lovers.

I slip, I slide, I gloom, I glance,
   Among my skimming swallows;
I make the netted sunbeam dance
   Against my sandy shallows.

I murmur under moon and stars
   In brambly wildernesses;
I linger by my shingly bars;
   I loiter round my cresses;

And out again I curve and flow
  To join the brimming river,
For men may come and men may go,
  But I go on for ever.

XX

THE DAISY

WRITTEN AT EDINBURGH

O LOVE, what hours were thine and mine,
In lands of palm and southern pine;
  In lands of palm, of orange-blossom,
Of olive, aloe, and maize and vine.

What Roman strength Turbìa show'd
In ruin, by the mountain road;
  How like a gem, beneath, the city
Of little Monaco, basking, glow'd.

How richly down the rocky dell
The torrent vineyard streaming fell
  To meet the sun and sunny waters,
That only heaved with a summer swell.

What slender campanili grew
By bays, the peacock's neck in hue;
  Where, here and there, on sandy beaches
A milky-bell'd amaryllis blew.

How young Columbus seem'd to rove,
Yet present in his natal grove,
  Now watching high on mountain cornice,
And steering, now, from a purple cove,

Now pacing mute by ocean's rim;
Till, in a narrow street and dim,
  I stay'd the wheels at Cogoletto,
And drank, and loyally drank to him.

Nor knew we well what pleased us most,
Not the clipt palm of which they boast;
   But distant colour, happy hamlet,
A moulder'd citadel on the coast,

Or tower, or high hill-convent, seen
A light amid its olives green;
   Or olive-hoary cape in ocean;
Or rosy blossom in hot ravine,

Where oleanders flush'd the bed
Of silent torrents, gravel-spread;
   And, crossing, oft we saw the glisten
Of ice, far up on a mountain head.

We loved that hall, tho' white and cold,
Those niched shapes of noble mould,
   A princely people's awful princes,
The grave, severe Genovese of old.

At Florence too what golden hours,
In those long galleries, were ours;
   What drives about the fresh Cascinè,
Or walks in Boboli's ducal bowers.

In bright vignettes, and each complete,
Of tower or duomo, sunny-sweet,
   Or palace, how the city glitter'd,
Thro' cypress avenues, at our feet.

But when we crost the Lombard plain
Remember what a plague of rain;
   Of rain at Reggio, rain at Parma;
At Lodi, rain, Piacenza, rain.

And stern and sad (so rare the smiles
Of sunlight) look'd the Lombard piles;
   Porch-pillars on the lion resting,
And sombre, old, colonnaded aisles.

O Milan, O the chanting quires,
The giant windows' blazon'd fires,
   The height, the space, the gloom, the glory!
A mount of marble, a hundred spires!

I climb'd the roofs at break of day;
Sun-smitten Alps before me lay.
   I stood among the silent statues,
And statued pinnacles, mute as they.

How faintly-flush'd, how phantom-fair,
Was Monte Rosa, hanging there
   A thousand shadowy-pencill'd valleys
And snowy dells in a golden air.

Remember how we came at last
To Como; shower and storm and blast
   Had blown the lake beyond his limit,
And all was flooded; and how we past

From Como, when the light was gray,
And in my head, for half the day,
   The rich Virgilian rustic measure
Of Lari Maxume, all the way,

Like ballad-burthen music, kept,
As on The Lariano crept
   To that fair port below the castle
Of Queen Theodolind, where we slept;

Or hardly slept, but watch'd awake
A cypress in the moonlight shake,
   The moonlight touching o'er a terrace
One tall Agavè above the lake.

What more? we took our last adieu,
And up the snowy Splugen drew,
   But ere we reach'd the highest summit
I pluck'd a daisy, I gave it you.

It told of England then to me,
And now it tells of Italy.
   O love, we two shall go no longer
To lands of summer across the sea;

So dear a life your arms enfold
Whose crying is a cry for gold:
   Yet here to-night in this dark city,
When ill and weary, alone and cold,

I found, tho' crush'd to hard and dry,
This nurseling of another sky
   Still in the little book you lent me,
And where you tenderly laid it by:

And I forgot the clouded Forth,
The gloom that saddens Heaven and Earth,
   The bitter east, the misty summer
And gray metropolis of the North.

Perchance, to lull the throbs of pain,
Perchance, to charm a vacant brain,
   Perchance, to dream you still beside me,
My fancy fled to the South again.

XXI

TO THE REV. F. D. MAURICE

COME, when no graver cares employ,
Godfather, come and see your boy:
   Your presence will be sun in winter,
Making the little one leap for joy.

For, being of that honest few,
Who give the Fiend himself his due,
   Should eighty-thousand college-councils
Thunder 'Anathema,' friend, at you;

Should all our churchmen foam in spite
At you, so careful of the right,
   Yet one lay-hearth would give you welcome
(Take it and come) to the Isle of Wight;

Where, far from noise and smoke of town,
I watch the twilight falling brown
   All round a careless-order'd garden
Close to the ridge of a noble down.

You'll have no scandal while you dine,
But honest talk and wholesome wine,
   And only hear the magpie gossip
Garrulous under a roof of pine:

For groves of pine on either hand,
To break the blast of winter, stand ;
   And further on, the hoary Channel
Tumbles a billow on chalk and sand ;

Where, if below the milky steep
Some ship of battle slowly creep,
   And on thro' zones of light and shadow
Glimmer away to the lonely deep,

We might discuss the Northern sin
Which made a selfish war begin ;
   Dispute the claims, arrange the chances ;
Emperor, Ottoman, which shall win :

Or whether war's avenging rod
Shall lash all Europe into blood ;
   Till you should turn to dearer matters,
Dear to the man that is dear to God ;

How best to help the slender store,
How mend the dwellings, of the poor ;
   How gain in life, as life advances,
Valour and charity more and more.

Come, Maurice, come : the lawn as yet
Is hoar with rime, or spongy-wet ;
   But when the wreath of March has blossom'd,
Crocus, anemone, violet,

Or later, pay one visit here,
For those are few we hold as dear ;
   Nor pay but one, but come for many,
Many and many a happy year.

January, 1854

XXII
NORTHERN FARMER
OLD STYLE

I

Wheer 'asta beän saw long and meä liggin' 'ere aloän?
Noorse? thoort nowt o' a noorse: whoy, Doctor's abeän an' agoän:
Says that I moänt 'a naw moor aäle: but I beänt a fool:
Git ma my aäle, fur I beänt a-gooin' to breäk my rule.

II

Doctors, they knaws nowt, fur a says what's nawways true:
Naw soort o' koind o' use to saäy the things that a do.
I've 'ed my point o' aäle ivry noight sin' I beän 'ere,
An' I've 'ed my quart ivry market-noight for foorty year.

III

Parson's a beän loikewoise, an' a sittin' ere o' my bed.
'The amoighty's a taäkin o' you to 'issén, my friend,' a said,
An' a towd ma my sins, an's toithe were due, an' I gied it in hond;
I done moy duty boy 'um, as I 'a done boy the lond.

IV

Larn'd a ma' beä. I reckons I 'annot sa mooch to larn.
But a cast oop, thot a did, 'boot Bessy Marris's barne.
Thaw a knaws I hallus voäted wi' Squoire an' choorch an' staäte,
An' i' the woost o' toimes I wur niver agin the raäte.

V

An' I hallus coom'd to 's choorch afoor moy Sally wur deäd,
An' 'eerd 'um a bummin' awaäy loike a buzzard-clock [1] ower my 'eäd,
An' I niver knaw'd whot a meän'd but I thowt a 'ad summut to saäy,
An' I thowt a said whot a owt to 'a said an' I coom'd awaäy.

VI

Bessy Marris's barne! tha knaws she laäid it to meä.
Mowt a beän, mayhap, for she wur a bad un, sheä.
'Siver, I kep 'um, I kep 'um, my lass, tha mun understond;
I done moy duty boy 'um as I 'a done boy the lond.

VII

But Parson a cooms an' a goos, an' a says it eäsy an' freeä
'The amoighty's a taäkin o' you to 'issén, my friend,' says 'eä.
I weänt saäy men be loiars, thaw summun said it in 'aäste:
But 'e reäds wonn sarmin a weeäk, an' I 'a stubb'd Thurnaby waäste.

VIII

D'ya moind the waäste, my lass? naw, naw, tha was not born then;
Theer wur a boggle in it, I often 'eerd 'um mysen;
Moäst loike a butter-bump,[2] fur I 'eerd 'um aboot an' aboot,
But I stubb'd 'um oop wi' the lot, an' raäved an' rembled 'um oot.

[1] Cockchafer. [2] Bittern.

IX

Keäper's it wur; fo' they fun 'um theer a-laäid of 'is faäce
Doon i' the woild 'enemies[1] afoor I coom'd to the plaäce.
Noäks or Thimbleby—toäner 'ed shot 'um as deäd as a naäil.
Noäks wur 'ang'd for it oop at 'soize—but git ma my aäle.

X

Dubbut loook at the waäste: theer warn't not feeäd for a cow;
Nowt at all but bracken an' fuzz, an' loook at it now—
Warnt worth nowt a haäcre, an' now theer's lots o' feeäd,
Fourscoor yows upon it an' some on it doon i' seeäd.

XI

Nobbut a bit on it's left, an' I meän'd to 'a stubb'd it at fall,
Done it ta-year I meän'd, an' runn'd plow thruff it an' all,
If godamoighty an' parson 'ud nobbut let ma aloän,
Meä, wi' haäte oonderd haäcre o' Squoire's, an' lond o' my oän.

XII

Do godamoighty knaw what a's doing a-taäkin' o' meä?
I beänt wonn as saws 'ere a beän an' yonder a peä;
An' Squoire 'ull be sa mad an' all—a' dear a' dear!
And I 'a managed for Squoire coom Michaelmas thutty year.

XIII

A mowt 'a taäen owd Joänes, as 'ant nor a 'aäpoth o' sense,
Or a mowt 'a taäen young Robins—a niver mended a fence:

[1] Anemones.

But godamoighty a moost taäke meä an' taäke ma now
Wi' aäf the cows to cauve an' Thurnaby hoälms to
    plow!

XIV

Loook 'ow quoloty smoiles when they seeäs ma a passin'
    boy,
Says to thessén naw doubt 'what a man a beä sewer-
    loy!'
Fur they knaws what I beän to Squoire sin fust a
    coom'd to the 'All;
I done moy duty by Squoire an' I done moy duty boy
    hall.

XV

Squoire's i' Lunnon, an' summun I reckons 'ull 'a to
    wroite,
For whoä's to howd the lond ater meä thot muddles
    ma quoit;
Sartin-sewer I beä, thot a weänt niver give it to Joänes,
Naw, nor a moänt to Robins—a niver rembles the
    stoäns.

XVI

But summun 'ull come ater meä mayhap wi' 'is kittle
    o' steäm
Huzzin' an' maäzin' the blessed feälds wi' the Divil's
    oän teäm.
Sin' I mun doy I mun doy, thaw loife they says is sweet,
But sin' I mun doy I mun doy, for I couldn abeär to
    see it.

XVII

What atta stannin' theer fur, an' doesn bring ma the
    aäle?
Doctor's a 'toättler, lass, an a's hallus i' the owd taäle;
I weänt breäk rules fur Doctor, a knaws naw moor
    nor a floy;
Git ma my aäle I tell tha, an' if I mun doy I mun doy.

I

XXIII
NORTHERN FARMER
NEW STYLE

I

Dosn't thou 'ear my 'erse's legs, as they canters awaäy?
Proputty, proputty, proputty—that's what I 'ears 'em saäy.
Proputty, proputty, proputty—Sam, thou's an ass for thy paaïns:
Theer's moor sense i' one o' 'is legs nor in all thy braaïns.

II

Woä—theer's a craw to pluck wi' tha, Sam: yon's parson's 'ouse—
Dosn't thou knaw that a man mun be eäther a man or a mouse?
Time to think on it then; for thou'll be twenty to weeäk.[1]
Proputty, proputty—woä then woä—let ma 'ear mysén speäk.

III

Me an' thy muther, Sammy, 'as beän a-talkin' o' thee;
Thou's beän talkin' to muther, an' she beän a tellin' it me.
Thou'll not marry for munny—thou's sweet upo' parson's lass—
Noä—thou'll marry for luvv—an' we boäth on us thinks tha an ass.

IV

Seeä'd her todaäy goä by—Saäint's-daäy—they was ringing the bells.
She's a beauty thou thinks—an' soä is scoors o' gells,

[1] This week.

Them as 'as munny an' all—wot's a beauty?—the flower as blaws.
But proputty, proputty sticks, an' proputty, proputty graws.

V

Do'ant be stunt:[1] taäke time: I knaws what maäkes tha sa mad.
Warn't I craäzed fur the lasses mysén when I wur a lad?
But I knaw'd a Quaäker feller as often 'as towd ma this:
'Doänt thou marry for munny, but goä wheer munny is!'

VI

An' I went wheer munny war: an' thy muther coom to 'and,
Wi' lots o' munny laaïd by, an' a nicetish bit o' land.
Maäybe she warn't a beauty:—I niver giv it a thowt—
But warn't she as good to cuddle an' kiss as a lass as 'ant nowt?

VII

Parson's lass ant nowt, an' she weänt 'a nowt when 'e's deäd,
Mun be a guvness, lad, or summut, and addle[2] her breäd:
Why? fur 'e's nobbut a curate, an' weänt niver git naw 'igher;
An' 'e maäde the bed as 'e ligs on afoor 'e coom'd to the shire.

VIII

An thin 'e coom'd to the parish wi' lots o' Varsity debt,
Stook to his taaïl they did, an' 'e 'ant got shut on 'em yet.

[1] Obstinate. [2] Earn.

An' 'e ligs on 'is back i' the grip, wi' noän to lend 'im a shove,
Woorse nor a far-welter'd[1] yowe: fur, Sammy, 'e married fur luvv.

IX

Luvv? what's luvv? thou can luvv thy lass an' 'er munny too,
Maakin' 'em goä togither as they've good right to do.
Could'n I luvv thy muther by cause o' 'er munny laaïd by?
Naäy—fur I luvv'd 'er a vast sight moor fur it: reäson why.

X

Ay an' thy muther says thou wants to marry the lass,
Cooms of a gentleman burn: an' we boäth on us thinks tha an ass.
Woä then, proputty, wiltha?—an ass as near as mays nowt[2]—
Woä then, wiltha? dangtha!—the bees is as fell as owt.[3]

XI

Breäk me a bit o' the esh for his 'eäd, lad, out o' the fence!
Gentleman burn! what's gentleman burn? is it shillins an' pence?
Proputty, proputty's ivrything 'ere, an', Sammy, I'm blest
If it isn't the saäme oop yonder, fur them as 'as it's the best.

XII

Tis'n them as 'as munny as breäks into 'ouses an' steäls,
Them as 'as coäts to their backs an' taäkes their regular meäls.

---

[1] Or fow-welter'd,—said of a sheep lying on its back in the furrow.
[2] Makes nothing.
[3] The flies are as fierce as anything.

Noä, but it's them as niver knaws wheer a meäl's to be 'ad.
Taäke my word for it, Sammy, the poor in a loomp is bad.

XIII

Them or thir feythers, tha sees, mun 'a beän a laäzy lot,
Fur work mun 'a gone to the gittin' whiniver munny was got.
Feyther 'ad ammost nowt; leästways 'is munny was 'id.
But 'e tued an' moil'd 'issén deäd, an 'e died a good un, 'e did.

XIV

Loook thou theer wheer Wrigglesby beck cooms out by the 'ill!
Feyther run oop to the farm, an' I runs oop to the mill;
An' I'll run oop to the brig, an' that thou'll live to see;
And if thou marries a good un I'll leäve the land to thee.

XV

Thim's my noätions, Sammy, wheerby I means to stick;
But if thou marries a bad un, I'll leäve the land to Dick.—
Coom oop, proputty, proputty—that's what I 'ears 'im saäy—
Proputty, proputty, proputty—canter an' canter awaäy.

XXIV

THE NORTHERN COBBLER

I

Waäit till our Sally cooms in, fur thou mun a' sights[1] to tell.
Eh, but I be maäin glad to seeä tha sa 'arty an' well.
'Cast awaäy on a disolut land wi' a vartical soon[2]!'
Strange fur to goä fur to think what saäilors a' seëan an' a' doon;
'Summat to drink—sa' 'ot?' I 'a nowt but Adam's wine:
What's the 'eät o' this little 'ill-side to the 'eät o' the line?

II

'What's i' tha bottle a-stanning theer?' I'll tell tha. Gin.
But if thou wants thy grog, tha mun goä fur it down to the inn.
Naay—fur I be maäin-glad, but thaw tha was iver sa dry,
Thou gits naw gin fro' the bottle theer, an' I'll tell tha why.

III

Meä an' thy sister was married, when wur it? back-end o' June,
Ten year sin', and wa 'greed as well as a fiddle i' tune:
I could fettle and clump owd booöts and shoes wi' the best on 'em all,
As fer as fro' Thursby thurn hup to Harmsby and Hutterby Hall.

---

[1] The vowels *aï*, pronounced separately though in the closest conjunction, best render the sound of the long *i* and *y* in this dialect. But since such words as *craïin'*, *daïin'*, *whaï*, *aï* (I), etc., look awkward except in a page of express phonetics, I have thought it better to leave the simple *i* and *y*, and to trust that my readers will give them the broader pronunciation.

[2] The *oo* short, as in 'wood.'

We was busy as beeäs i' the bloom an' as 'appy as 'art
   could think,
An' then the babby wur burn, and then I taäkes to
   the drink.

IV

An' I weänt gaäinsaäy it, my lad, thaw I be hafe
   shaämed on it now,
We could sing a good song at the Plow, we could sing
   a good song at the Plow;
Thaw once of a frosty night I slither'd an' hurted my
   huck,[1]
An' I coom'd neck-an-crop soomtimes slaäpe down i'
   the squad an' the muck:
An' once I fowt wi' the Taäilor—not hafe ov a man,
   my lad—
Fur he scrawm'd an' scratted my faäce like a cat, an'
   it maäde 'er sa mad
That Sally she turn'd a tongue-banger,[2] an' raäted ma,
   ' Sottin' thy braäins
Guzzlin' an' soäkin' an' smoäkin' an' hawmin'[3] about
   i' the laänes,
Soä sow-droonk that tha doesn not touch thy 'at to the
   Squire;'
An' I looök'd cock-eyed at my noäse an' I seeäd 'im
   a-gittin' o' fire;
But sin' I wur hallus i' liquor an' hallus as droonk as a
   king,
Foälks' coostom flitted awaäy like a kite wi' a brokken
   string.

V

An' Sally she wesh'd foälks' cloäths to keep the wolf
   fro' the door,
Eh but the moor she riled me, she druv me to drink
   the moor,
Fur I fun', when 'er back wur turn'd, wheer Sally's
   owd stockin' wur 'id,
An' I grabb'd the munny she maäde, and I weär'd it
   o' liquor, I did.

---

[1] Hip.   [2] Scold.   [3] Lounging.

VI

An' one night I cooms 'oäm like a bull gotten loose at a faäir,
An' she wur a-waäitin' fo'mma, an' cryin' and teärin' 'er 'aäir,
An' I tummled athurt the craädle an' sweär'd as I'd breäk ivry stick
O' furnitur 'ere i' the 'ouse, an' I gied our Sally a kick,
An' I mash'd the taäbles an' chairs, an' she an' the babby beäl'd,[1]
Fur I knaw'd naw moor what I did nor a mortal beäst o' the feäld.

VII

An' when I waäked i' the murnin' I seeäd that our Sally went laämed
Cos' o' the kick as I gied 'er, an' I wur dreädful ashaämed;
An' Sally wur sloomy[2] an' draggle taäil'd in an owd turn gown,
An' the babby's faäce wurn't wesh'd an' the 'ole 'ouse hupside down.

VIII

An' then I minded our Sally sa pratty an' neät an' sweeät,
Straät as a pole an' cleän as a flower fro' 'eäd to feeät:
An' then I minded the fust kiss I gied 'er by Thursby thurn;
Theer wur a lark a-singin' 'is best of a Sunday at murn,
Couldn't see 'im, we 'eärd 'im a-mountin' oop 'igher an' 'igher,
An' then 'e turn'd to the sun, an' 'e shined like a sparkle o' fire.
'Doesn't tha see 'im,' she axes, 'fur I can see 'im?' an' I
Seeäd nobbut the smile o' the sun as danced in 'er pratty blue eye;

---

[1] Bellowed, cried out. [2] Sluggish, out of spirits.

An' I says ' I mun gie tha a kiss,' an' Sally says ' Noä,
    thou moänt,'
But I gied 'er a kiss, an' then anoother, an' Sally says
    ' doänt !'

IX

An' when we coom'd into Meeätin', at fust she wur
    all in a tew,
But, arter, we sing'd the 'ymn togither like birds on a
    beugh ;
An' Muggins 'e preäch'd o' Hell-fire an' the loov o'
    God fur men,
An' then upo' coomin' awaäy Sally gied me a kiss ov
    'ersen.

X

Heer wur a fall fro' a kiss to a kick like Saätan as fell
Down out o' heaven i' Hell-fire—thaw theer's naw
    drinkin' i' Hell ;
Meä fur to kick our Sally as kep the wolf fro' the door,
All along o' the drink, fur I loov'd 'er as well as afoor.

XI

Sa like a graät num-cumpus I blubber'd awaäy o' the
    bed—
' Weänt niver do it naw moor ;' an' Sally looökt up
    an' she said,
' I'll upowd it[1] tha weänt ; thou'rt like the rest o' the
    men,
Thou'll goä sniffin' about the tap till tha does it agëan.
Theer's thy hennemy, man, an' I knaws, as knaws tha
    sa well,
That, if tha seeäs 'im an' smells 'im tha'll foller 'im
    slick into Hell.'

XII

' Naäy,' says I, ' fur I weänt goä sniffin' about the tap.'
' Weänt tha ?' she says, an' mysen I thowt i' mysen
    ' mayhap.'

[1] I'll uphold it.

'Noä:' an' I started awaäy like a shot, an' down to the Hinn,
An' I browt what tha seeäs stannin' theer, yon big black bottle o' gin.

XIII

'That caps owt,'[1] says Sally, an' saw she begins to cry,
But I puts it inter 'er 'ands an' I says to 'er, 'Sally,' says I,
'Stan' 'im theer i' the naäme o' the Lord an' the power ov 'is Graäce,
Stan' 'im theer, fur I'll looök my hennemy straït i' the faäce,
Stan' 'im theer i' the winder, an' let ma looök at 'im then,
'E secäms naw moor nor watter, an' 'e's the Divil's oän sen.'

XIV

An' I wur down i' tha mouth, couldn't do naw work an' all,
Nasty an' snaggy an' shaäky, 'an poonch'd my 'and wi' the hawl,
But she wur a power o' coomfut, an' sattled 'ersen o' my knee,
An' coäxd an' coodled me oop till ageän I feel'd mysen free.

XV

An' Sally she tell'd it about, an' foälk stood a-gawmin'[2] in,
As thaw it wur summat bewitch'd istead of a quart o' gin ;
An' some on 'em said it wur watter—an' I wur chousin' the wife,
Fur I couldn't 'owd 'ands off gin, wur it nobbut to saäve my life ;
An' blacksmith 'e strips me the thick ov 'is airm, an' 'e shaws it to me,

---

[1] That's beyond everything.   [2] Staring vacantly.

'Feeäl thou this! thou can't graw this upo' watter!'
  says he.
An' Doctor 'e calls o' Sunday an' just as candles was
  lit,
'Thou moänt do it,' he says, 'tha mun breäk 'im off
  bit by bit.'
'Thou'rt but a Methody-man,' says Parson, and laäys
  down 'is 'at,
An' 'e points to the bottle o' gin, 'but I respecks tha
  fur that;'
An' Squire, his oän very sen, walks down fro' the 'All
  to see,
An' 'e spanks 'is 'and into mine, 'fur I respecks tha,'
  says 'e;
An' coostom ageän draw'd in like a wind fro' far
  an' wide,
And browt me the booöts to be cobbled fro' hafe the
  coontryside.

XVI

An' theer 'e stans an' theer 'e shall stan to my dying
  daäy;
I 'a gotten to loov 'im ageän in anoother kind of a
  waäy,
Proud on 'im, like, my lad, an' I keeäps 'im cleän
  an' bright,
Loovs 'im, an' roobs 'im, an' doosts 'im, an' puts 'im
  back i' the light.

XVII

Wouldn't a pint a' sarved as well as a quart? Naw
  doubt:
But I liked a bigger feller to fight wi' an' fowt it out.
Fine an' meller 'e mun be by this, if I cared to taäste,
But I moänt, my lad, and I weänt, fur I'd feäl mysen
  cleän disgraäced.

XVIII

An' once I said to the Missis, 'My lass, when I cooms
  to die,
Smash the bottle to smithers, the Divil's in 'im,'
  said I.

But arter I chaänged my mind, an' if Sally be left aloän,
I'll hev 'im a-buried wi'mma an' taäke 'im afoor the Throän.

XIX

Coom thou 'eer—yon laädy a-steppin' along the streeät,
Doesn't tha knaw 'er—sa pratty, an' feät, an' neät, an' sweeät?
Look at the cloäths on 'er back, thebbe ammost spick-span-new,
An' Tommy's faäce be as fresh as a codlin wesh'd i' the dew.

XX

'Ere be our Sally an' Tommy, an' we be a-goin' to dine,
Baäcon an taätes, an' a besling's-puddin'¹ an' Adam's wine;
But if tha wants ony grog tha mun goä fur it down to the Hinn,
Fur I weänt shed a drop on 'is blood, noä, not fur Sally's oän kin.

XXV

WILL WATERPROOF'S LYRICAL MONOLOGUE

MADE AT THE COCK

O PLUMP head-waiter at The Cock,
   To which I most resort,
How goes the time? 'Tis five o'clock.
   Go fetch a pint of port:
But let it not be such as that
   You set before chance-comers,
But such whose father-grape grew fat
   On Lusitanian summers.

---

¹ A pudding made with the first milk of the cow after calving.

No vain libation to the Muse,
  But may she still be kind,
And whisper lovely words, and use
  Her influence on the mind,
To make me write my random rhymes,
  Ere they be half-forgotten;
Nor add and alter, many times,
  Till all be ripe and rotten.

I pledge her, and she comes and dips
  Her laurel in the wine,
And lays it thrice upon my lips,
  These favour'd lips of mine;
Until the charm have power to make
  New lifeblood warm the bosom,
And barren commonplaces break
  In full and kindly blossom.

I pledge her silent at the board;
  Her gradual fingers steal
And touch upon the master-chord
  Of all I felt and feel.
Old wishes, ghosts of broken plans,
  And phantom hopes assemble;
And that child's heart within the man's
  Begins to move and tremble.

Thro' many an hour of summer suns,
  By many pleasant ways,
Against its fountain upward runs
  The current of my days:
I kiss the lips I once have kiss'd;
  The gas-light wavers dimmer;
And softly, thro' a vinous mist,
  My college friendships glimmer.

I grow in worth, and wit, and sense,
  Unboding critic-pen,
Or that eternal want of pence,
  Which vexes public men,
Who hold their hands to all, and cry
  For that which all deny them—
Who sweep the crossings, wet or dry,
  And all the world go by them.

Ah yet, tho' all the world forsake,
    Tho' fortune clip my wings,
I will not cramp my heart, nor take
    Half-views of men and things.
Let Whig and Tory stir their blood;
    There must be stormy weather;
But for some true result of good
    All parties work together.

Let there be thistles, there are grapes;
    If old things, there are new;
Ten thousand broken lights and shapes,
    Yet glimpses of the true.
Let raffs be rife in prose and rhyme,
    We lack not rhymes and reasons,
As on this whirligig of Time
    We circle with the seasons.

This earth is rich in man and maid;
    With fair horizons bound:
This whole wide earth of light and shade
    Comes out a perfect round.
High over roaring Temple-bar,
    And set in Heaven's third story,
I look at all things as they are,
    But thro' a kind of glory.

Head-waiter, honour'd by the guest
    Half-mused, or reeling ripe,
The pint, you brought me, was the best
    That ever came from pipe.
But tho' the port surpasses praise,
    My nerves have dealt with stiffer.
Is there some magic in the place?
    Or do my peptics differ?

For since I came to live and learn,
    No pint of white or red
Had ever half the power to turn
    This wheel within my head,

Which bears a season'd brain about,
  Unsubject to confusion,
Tho' soak'd and saturate, out and out,
  Thro' every convolution.

For I am of a numerous house,
  With many kinsmen gay,
Where long and largely we carouse
  As who shall say me nay:
Each month, a birth-day coming on,
  We drink defying trouble,
Or sometimes two would meet in one,
  And then we drank it double;

Whether the vintage, yet unkept,
  Had relish fiery-new,
Or elbow-deep in sawdust, slept,
  As old as Waterloo;
Or stow'd, when classic Canning died,
  In musty bins and chambers,
Had cast upon its crusty side
  The gloom of ten Decembers.

The Muse, the jolly Muse, it is!
  She answer'd to my call,
She changes with that mood or this,
  Is all-in-all to all:
She lit the spark within my throat,
  To make my blood run quicker,
Used all her fiery will, and smote
  Her life into the liquor.

And hence this halo lives about
  The waiter's hands, that reach
To each his perfect pint of stout,
  His proper chop to each.
He looks not like the common breed
  That with the napkin dally;
I think he came, like Ganymede,
  From some delightful valley.

The Cock was of a larger egg
  Than modern poultry drop,
Stept forward on a firmer leg,
  And cramm'd a plumper crop;
Upon an ampler dunghill trod,
  Crow'd lustier late and early,
Sipt wine from silver, praising God,
  And raked in golden barley.

A private life was all his joy,
  Till in a court he saw
A something-pottle-bodied boy
  That knuckled at the taw:
He stoop'd and clutch'd him, fair and good,
  Flew over roof and casement:
His brothers of the weather stood
  Stock-still for sheer amazement.

But he, by farmstead, thorpe and spire,
  And follow'd with acclaims,
A sign to many a staring shire
  Came crowing over Thames.
Right down by smoky Paul's they bore,
  Till, where the street grows straiter,
One fix'd for ever at the door,
  And one became head-waiter.

But whither would my fancy go?
  How out of place she makes
The violet of a legend blow
  Among the chops and steaks!
'Tis but a steward of the can,
  One shade more plump than common;
As just and mere a serving-man
  As any born of woman.

I ranged too high: what draws me down
  Into the common day?
Is it the weight of that half-crown,
  Which I shall have to pay?

For, something duller than at first,
  Nor wholly comfortable,
I sit, my empty glass reversed,
  And thrumming on the table:

Half fearful that, with self at strife,
  I take myself to task;
Lest of the fulness of my life
  I leave an empty flask:
For I had hope, by something rare
  To prove myself a poet:
But, while I plan and plan, my hair
  Is gray before I know it.

So fares it since the years began,
  Till they be gather'd up;
The truth, that flies the flowing can,
  Will haunt the vacant cup:
And others' follies teach us not,
  Nor much their wisdom teaches;
And most, of sterling worth, is what
  Our own experience preaches.

Ah, let the rusty theme alone!
  We know not what we know.
But for my pleasant hour, 'tis gone;
  'Tis gone, and let it go.
'Tis gone: a thousand such have slipt
  Away from my embraces,
And fall'n into the dusty crypt
  Of darken'd forms and faces.

Go, therefore, thou! thy betters went
  Long since, and came no more;
With peals of genial clamour sent
  From many a tavern-door,
With twisted quirks and happy hits,
  From misty men of letters;
The tavern-hours of mighty wits—
  Thine elders and thy betters.

Hours, when the Poet's words and looks
    Had yet their native glow:
Nor yet the fear of little books
    Had made him talk for show;
But, all his vast heart sherris-warm'd,
    He flash'd his random speeches,
Ere days, that deal in ana, swarm'd
    His literary leeches.

So mix for ever with the past,
    Like all good things on earth!
For should I prize thee, couldst thou last,
    At half thy real worth?
I hold it good, good things should pass:
    With time I will not quarrel:
It is but yonder empty glass
    That makes me maudlin-moral.

Head-waiter of the chop-house here,
    To which I most resort,
I too must part: I hold thee dear
    For this good pint of port.
For this, thou shalt from all things suck
    Marrow of mirth and laughter;
And wheresoe'er thou move, good luck
    Shall fling her old shoe after.

But thou wilt never move from hence,
    The sphere thy fate allots:
Thy latter days increased with pence
    Go down among the pots:
Thou battenest by the greasy gleam
    In haunts of hungry sinners,
Old boxes, larded with the steam
    Of thirty thousand dinners.

We fret, we fume, would shift our skins,
    Would quarrel with our lot;
Thy care is, under polish'd tins,
    To serve the hot-and-hot;

To come and go, and come again,
  Returning like the pewit,
And watch'd by silent gentlemen,
  That trifle with the cruet.

Live long, ere from thy topmost head
  The thick-set hazel dies;
Long, ere the hateful crow shall tread
  The corners of thine eyes:
Live long, nor feel in head or chest
  Our changeful equinoxes,
Till mellow Death, like some late guest,
  Shall call thee from the boxes.

But when he calls, and thou shalt cease
  To pace the gritted floor,
And, laying down an unctuous lease
  Of life, shalt earn no more;
No carved cross-bones, the types of Death,
  Shall show thee past to Heaven:
But carved cross-pipes, and, underneath,
  A pint-pot neatly graven.

XXVI

THE POET'S SONG

The rain had fallen, the Poet arose,
  He pass'd by the town and out of the street,
A light wind blew from the gates of the sun,
  And waves of shadow went over the wheat,
And he sat him down in a lonely place,
  And chanted a melody loud and sweet,
That made the wild-swan pause in her cloud,
  And the lark drop down at his feet.

The swallow stopt as he hunted the bee,
  The snake slipt under a spray,
The wild hawk stood with the down on his beak,
  And stared, with his foot on the prey,

And the nightingale thought, 'I have sung many songs,
  But never a one so gay,
For he sings of what the world will be
  When the years have died away.'

XXVII

TO ——,

AFTER READING A LIFE AND LETTERS

'Cursed be he that moves my bones.'
Shakespeare's Epitaph

You might have won the Poet's name,
  If such be worth the winning now,
  And gain'd a laurel for your brow
Of sounder leaf than I can claim;

But you have made the wiser choice,
  A life that moves to gracious ends
  Thro' troops of unrecording friends,
A deedful life, a silent voice:

And you have miss'd the irreverent doom
  Of those that wear the Poet's crown:
  Hereafter, neither knave nor clown
Shall hold their orgies at your tomb.

For now the Poet cannot die,
  Nor leave his music as of old,
  But round him ere he scarce be cold
Begins the scandal and the cry:

'Proclaim the faults he would not show:
  Break lock and seal: betray the trust:
  Keep nothing sacred: 'tis but just
The many-headed beast should know.'

Ah shameless! for he did but sing
  A song that pleased us from its worth;
  No public life was his on earth,
No blazon'd statesman he, nor king.

He gave the people of his best:
  His worst he kept, his best he gave.
  My Shakespeare's curse on clown and knave
Who will not let his ashes rest!

Who make it seem more sweet to be
  The little life of bank and brier,
  The bird that pipes his lone desire
And dies unheard within his tree,

Than he that warbles long and loud
  And drops at Glory's temple-gates,
  For whom the carrion vulture waits
To tear his heart before the crowd!

XXVIII

ALCAICS

O MIGHTY-MOUTH'D inventor of harmonies,
O skill'd to sing of Time or Eternity,
  God-gifted organ-voice of England,
    Milton, a name to resound for ages;
Whose Titan angels, Gabriel, Abdiel,
Starr'd from Jehovah's gorgeous armouries,
  Tower, as the deep-domed empyrëan
    Rings to the roar of an angel onset—
Me rather all that bowery loneliness,
The brooks of Eden mazily murmuring,
  And bloom profuse and cedar arches
    Charm, as a wanderer out in ocean,
Where some refulgent sunset of India
Streams o'er a rich ambrosial ocean isle,
  And crimson-hued the stately palm-woods
    Whisper in odorous heights of even.

XXIX

THE LADY OF SHALOTT

PART I

On either side the river lie
Long fields of barley and of rye,
That clothe the wold and meet the sky;
And thro' the field the road runs by
    To many-tower'd Camelot;
And up and down the people go,
Gazing where the lilies blow
Round an island there below,
    The island of Shalott.

Willows whiten, aspens quiver,
Little breezes dusk and shiver
Thro' the wave that runs for ever
By the island in the river
    Flowing down to Camelot.
Four gray walls, and four gray towers,
Overlook a space of flowers,
And the silent isle imbowers
    The Lady of Shalott.

By the margin, willow-veil'd,
Slide the heavy barges trail'd
By slow horses; and unhail'd
The shallop flitteth silken-sail'd
    Skimming down to Camelot:
But who hath seen her wave her hand?
Or at the casement seen her stand?
Or is she known in all the land,
    The Lady of Shalott?

Only reapers, reaping early
In among the bearded barley,
Hear a song that echoes cheerly
From the river winding clearly,
    Down to tower'd Camelot:
And by the moon the reaper weary,
Piling sheaves in uplands airy,
Listening, whispers ''Tis the fairy
    Lady of Shalott.'

Or whe
Came tw
' I am hal
   The

She left the web, she left the loom,
She made three paces thro' the room,
She saw the water-lily bloom,
She saw the helmet and the plume,
      She look'd down to Camelot.
Out flew the web and floated wide;
The mirror crack'd from side to side;
'The curse is come upon me,' cried
      The Lady of Shalott.

PART IV

IN the stormy east-wind straining,
The pale yellow woods were waning,
The broad stream in his banks complaining,
Heavily the low sky raining
      Over tower'd Camelot;
Down she came and found a boat
Beneath a willow left afloat,
And round about the prow she wrote
      The Lady of Shalott.

And down the river's dim expanse
Like some bold seër in a trance,
Seeing all his own mischance—
With a glassy countenance
      Did she look to Camelot.
And at the closing of the day
She loosed the chain, and down she lay;
The broad stream bore her far away,
      The Lady of Shalott.

Lying, robed in snowy white
That loosely flew to left and right—
The leaves upon her falling light—
Thro' the noises of the night
      She floated down to Camelot:
And as the boat-head wound along
The willowy hills and fields among,
They heard her singing her last song,
      The Lady of Shalott.

Heard a carol, mournful, holy,
Chanted loudly, chanted lowly,
Till her blood was frozen slowly,
And her eyes were darken'd wholly,
    Turn'd to tower'd Camelot.
For ere she reach'd upon the tide
The first house by the water-side,
Singing in her song she died,
    The Lady of Shalott.

Under tower and balcony,
By garden-wall and gallery,
A gleaming shape she floated by,
Dead-pale between the houses high,
    Silent into Camelot.
Out upon the wharfs they came,
Knight and burgher, lord and dame,
And round the prow they read her name,
    The Lady of Shalott.

Who is this? and what is here?
And in the lighted palace near
Died the sound of royal cheer;
And they cross'd themselves for fear,
    All the knights at Camelot:
But Lancelot mused a little space;
He said, 'She has a lovely face;
God in his mercy lend her grace,
    The Lady of Shalott.'

XXX

SIR LAUNCELOT AND QUEEN GUINEVERE

A FRAGMENT

LIKE souls that balance joy and pain,
With tears and smiles from heaven again
The maiden Spring upon the plain
Came in a sun-lit fall of rain.

In crystal vapour everywhere
Blue isles of heaven laugh'd between,
And far, in forest-deeps unseen,
The topmost elm-tree gather'd green
    From draughts of balmy air.

Sometimes the linnet piped his song :
Sometimes the throstle whistled strong :
Sometimes the sparhawk, wheel'd along,
Hush'd all the groves from fear of wrong :
    By grassy capes with fuller sound
In curves the yellowing river ran,
And drooping chestnut-buds began
To spread into the perfect fan,
    Above the teeming ground.

Then, in the boyhood of the year,
Sir Launcelot and Queen Guinevere
Rode thro' the coverts of the deer,
With blissful treble ringing clear.
    She seem'd a part of joyous Spring :
A gown of grass-green silk she wore,
Buckled with golden clasps before ;
A light-green tuft of plumes she bore
    Closed in a golden ring.

Now on some twisted ivy-net,
Now by some tinkling rivulet,
In mosses mixt with violet
Her cream-white mule his pastern set :
    And fleeter now she skimm'd the plains
Than she whose elfin prancer springs
By night to eery warblings,
When all the glimmering moorland rings
    With jingling bridle-reins.

As she fled fast thro' sun and shade,
The happy winds upon her play'd,
Blowing the ringlet from the braid :
She look'd so lovely, as she sway'd

      The rein with dainty finger-tips,
A man had given all other bliss,
And all his worldly worth for this,
To waste his whole heart in one kiss
      Upon her perfect lips.

XXXI

SIR GALAHAD

My good blade carves the casques of men,
    My tough lance thrusteth sure,
My strength is as the strength of ten,
    Because my heart is pure.
The shattering trumpet shrilleth high,
    The hard brands shiver on the steel,
The splinter'd spear-shafts crack and fly,
    The horse and rider reel :
They reel, they roll in clanging lists,
    And when the tide of combat stands,
Perfume and flowers fall in showers,
    That lightly rain from ladies' hands.

How sweet are looks that ladies bend
    On whom their favours fall !
For them I battle till the end,
    To save from shame and thrall :
But all my heart is drawn above,
    My knees are bow'd in crypt and shrine :
I never felt the kiss of love,
    Nor maiden's hand in mine.
More bounteous aspects on me beam,
    Me mightier transports move and thrill ;
So keep I fair thro' faith and prayer
    A virgin heart in work and will.

When down the stormy crescent goes,
    A light before me swims,
Between dark stems the forest glows,
    I hear a noise of hymns :
Then by some secret shrine I ride ;
    I hear a voice but none are there ;

The stalls are void, the doors are wide,
    The tapers burning fair.
Fair gleams the snowy altar-cloth,
    The silver vessels sparkle clean,
The shrill bell rings, the censer swings,
    And solemn chaunts resound between.

Sometimes on lonely mountain-meres
    I find a magic bark;
I leap on board: no helmsman steers:
    I float till all is dark.
A gentle sound, an awful light!
    Three angels bear the holy Grail:
With folded feet, in stoles of white,
    On sleeping wings they sail.
Ah, blessed vision! blood of God!
    My spirit beats her mortal bars,
As down dark tides the glory slides,
    And star-like mingles with the stars.

When on my goodly charger borne
    Thro' dreaming towns I go,
The cock crows ere the Christmas morn,
    The streets are dumb with snow.
The tempest crackles on the leads,
    And, ringing, springs from brand and mail;
But o'er the dark a glory spreads,
    And gilds the driving hail.
I leave the plain, I climb the height;
    No branchy thicket shelter yields;
But blessed forms in whistling storms
    Fly o'er waste fens and windy fields.

A maiden knight—to me is given
    Such hope, I know not fear;
I yearn to breathe the airs of heaven
    That often meet me here.
I muse on joy that will not cease,
    Pure spaces clothed in living beams,
Pure lilies of eternal peace,
    Whose odours haunt my dreams;
And, stricken by an angel's hand,
    This mortal armour that I wear,

This weight and size, this heart and eyes,
  Are touch'd, are turn'd to finest air.

The clouds are broken in the sky,
  And thro' the mountain-walls
A rolling organ-harmony
  Swells up, and shakes and falls.
Then move the trees, the copses nod,
  Wings flutter, voices hover clear:
'O just and faithful knight of God!
  Ride on! the prize is near.'
So pass I hostel, hall, and grange;
  By bridge and ford, by park and pale,
All-arm'd I ride, whate'er betide,
  Until I find the holy Grail.

XXXII

ST. AGNES' EVE

Deep on the convent-roof the snows
  Are sparkling to the moon:
My breath to heaven like vapour goes:
  May my soul follow soon!
The shadows of the convent-towers
  Slant down the snowy sward,
Still creeping with the creeping hours
  That lead me to my Lord:
Make Thou my spirit pure and clear
  As are the frosty skies,
Or this first snowdrop of the year
  That in my bosom lies.

As these white robes are soil'd and dark,
  To yonder shining ground;
As this pale taper's earthly spark,
  To yonder argent round;
So shows my soul before the Lamb,
  My spirit before Thee;
So in mine earthly house I am,
  To that I hope to be.

Break up the heavens, O Lord ! and far,
    Thro' all yon starlight keen,
Draw me, thy bride, a glittering star,
    In raiment white and clean.

He lifts me to the golden doors ;
    The flashes come and go ;
All heaven bursts her starry floors,
    And strows her lights below,
And deepens on and up ! the gates
    Roll back, and far within
For me the Heavenly Bridegroom waits,
    To make me pure of sin.
The sabbaths of Eternity,
    One sabbath deep and wide—
A light upon the shining sea—
    The Bridegroom with his bride !

XXXIII
A FAREWELL

Flow down, cold rivulet, to the sea,
    Thy tribute wave deliver :
No more by thee my steps shall be,
    For ever and for ever.

Flow, softly flow, by lawn and lea,
    A rivulet then a river :
No where by thee my steps shall be,
    For ever and for ever.

But here will sigh thine alder tree,
    And here thine aspen shiver ;
And here by thee will hum the bee,
    For ever and for ever.

A thousand suns will stream on thee,
    A thousand moons will quiver ;
But not by thee my steps shall be,
    For ever and for ever.

XXXIV

COME not, when I am dead,
   To drop thy foolish tears upon my grave,
To trample round my fallen head,
   And vex the unhappy dust thou wouldst not save.
There let the wind sweep and the plover cry;
   But thou, go by.

Child, if it were thine error or thy crime
   I care no longer, being all unblest:
Wed whom thou wilt, but I am sick of Time,
   And I desire to rest.
Pass on, weak heart, and leave me where I lie:
   Go by, go by.

XXXV

HAPLESS doom of woman happy in betrothing!
Beauty passes like a breath and love is lost in loathing:
Low, my lute; speak low, my lute, but say the world is nothing—
   Low, lute, low!

Love will hover round the flowers when they first awaken;
Love will fly the fallen leaf, and not be overtaken;
Low, my lute! oh low, my lute! we fade and are forsaken—
   Low, dear lute, low!

XXXVI

ASK me no more: the moon may draw the sea;
   The cloud may stoop from heaven and take the shape
   With fold to fold, of mountain or of cape;
But O too fond, when have I answer'd thee?
      Ask me no more.

Ask me no more: what answer should I give?
   I love not hollow cheek or faded eye:
   Yet, O my friend, I will not have thee die!
Ask me no more, lest I should bid thee live;
      Ask me no more.

Ask me no more: thy fate and mine are seal'd:
  I strove against the stream and all in vain:
  Let the great river take me to the main:
No more, dear love, for at a touch I yield;
              Ask me no more.

XXXVII

Sweet and low, sweet and low,
  Wind of the western sea,
Low, low, breathe and blow,
  Wind of the western sea!
Over the rolling waters go,
Come from the dying moon, and blow,
  Blow him again to me;
While my little one, while my pretty one, sleeps.

Sleep and rest, sleep and rest,
  Father will come to thee soon;
Rest, rest, on mother's breast,
  Father will come to thee soon;
Father will come to his babe in the nest,
Silver sails all out of the west
  Under the silver moon:
Sleep, my little one, sleep, my pretty one, sleep.

XXXVIII

What does little birdie say
In her nest at peep of day?
Let me fly, says little birdie,
Mother, let me fly away.
Birdie, rest a little longer,
Till the little wings are stronger.
So she rests a little longer,
Then she flies away.

What does little baby say,
In her bed at peep of day?
Baby says, like little birdie,
Let me rise and fly away.

Baby, sleep a little longer,
Till the little limbs are stronger.
If she sleeps a little longer,
Baby too shall fly away.

XXXIX

I

O LET the solid ground
   Not fail beneath my feet
Before my life has found
   What some have found so sweet;
Then let come what come may,
What matter if I go mad,
I shall have had my day.

II

Let the sweet heavens endure,
   Not close and darken above me
Before I am quite quite sure
   That there is one to love me;
Then let come what come may
To a life that has been so sad,
I shall have had my day.

XL.

I

BIRDS in the high Hall-garden
   When twilight was falling,
Maud, Maud, Maud, Maud,
   They were crying and calling.

II

Where was Maud? in our wood;
   And I, who else, was with her,
Gathering woodland lilies,
   Myriads blow together.

III

Birds in our wood sang
  Ringing thro' the valleys,
Maud is here, here, here
  In among the lilies.

IV

I kiss'd her slender hand,
  She took the kiss sedately;
Maud is not seventeen,
  But she is tall and stately.

V

I to cry out on pride
  Who have won her favour!
O Maud were sure of Heaven
  If lowliness could save her.

VI

I know the way she went
  Home with her maiden posy,
For her feet have touch'd the meadows
  And left the daisies rosy.

VII

Birds in the high Hall-garden
  Were crying and calling to her,
Where is Maud, Maud, Maud?
  One is come to woo her.

VIII

Look, a horse at the door,
  And little King Charley snarling,
Go back, my lord, across the moor,
  You are not her darling.

XLI

Go not, happy day,
  From the shining fields,
Go not, happy day,
  Till the maiden yields.

Rosy is the West,
  Rosy is the South,
Roses are her cheeks,
  And a rose her mouth
When the happy Yes
  Falters from her lips,
Pass and blush the news
  Over glowing ships;
Over blowing seas,
  Over seas at rest,
Pass the happy news,
  Blush it thro' the West;
Till the red man dance
  By his red cedar-tree,
And the red man's babe
  Leap, beyond the sea.
Blush from West to East,
  Blush from East to West,
Till the West is East,
  Blush it thro' the West.
Rosy is the West,
  Rosy is the South,
Roses are her cheeks,
  And a rose her mouth.

XLII

RIVULET crossing my ground,
And bringing me down from the Hall
This garden-rose that I found,
Forgetful of Maud and me,
And lost in trouble and moving round
Here at the head of a tinkling fall,
And trying to pass to the sea;
O Rivulet, born at the Hall,
My Maud has sent it by thee
(If I read her sweet will right)
On a blushing mission to me,
Saying in odour and colour, 'Ah, be
Among the roses to-night.'

XLIII

I

Come into the garden, Maud,
  For the black bat, night, has flown,
Come into the garden, Maud,
  I am here at the gate alone;
And the woodbine spices are wafted abroad,
  And the musk of the rose is blown.

II

For a breeze of morning moves,
  And the planet of Love is on high,
Beginning to faint in the light that she loves
  On a bed of daffodil sky,
To faint in the light of the sun she loves,
  To faint in his light, and to die.

III

All night have the roses heard
  The flute, violin, bassoon;
All night has the casement jessamine stirr'd
  To the dancers dancing in tune;
Till a silence fell with the waking bird,
  And a hush with the setting moon.

IV

I said to the lily, 'There is but one
  With whom she has heart to be gay.
When will the dancers leave her alone?
  She is weary of dance and play.'
Now half to the setting moon are gone,
  And half to the rising day;
Low on the sand and loud on the stone
  The last wheel echoes away.

V

I said to the rose, 'The brief night goes
  In babble and revel and wine.

O young lord-lover, what sighs are those,
  For one that will never be thine?
But mine, but mine,' so I sware to the rose,
  'For ever and ever, mine.'

VI

And the soul of the rose went into my blood,
  As the music clash'd in the hall;
And long by the garden lake I stood,
  For I heard your rivulet fall
From the lake to the meadow and on to the wood,
  Our wood, that is dearer than all;

VII

From the meadow your walks have left so sweet
  That whenever a March-wind sighs
He sets the jewel-print of your feet
  In violets blue as your eyes,
To the woody hollows in which we meet
  And the valleys of Paradise.

VIII

The slender acacia would not shake
  One long milk-bloom on the tree;
The white lake-blossom fell into the lake
  As the pimpernel dozed on the lea;
But the rose was awake all night for your sake,
  Knowing your promise to me;
The lilies and roses were all awake,
  They sigh'd for the dawn and thee.

IX

Queen rose of the rosebud garden of girls,
  Come hither, the dances are done,
In gloss of satin and glimmer of pearls,
  Queen lily and rose in one;
Shine out, little head, sunning over with curls,
  To the flowers, and be their sun.

X

There has fallen a splendid tear
  From the passion-flower at the gate.

She is coming, my dove, my dear;
   She is coming, my life, my fate;
The red rose cries, 'She is near, she is near;'
   And the white rose weeps, 'She is late;'
The larkspur listens, 'I hear, I hear;'
   And the lily whispers, 'I wait.'

XI

She is coming, my own, my sweet;
   Were it ever so airy a tread,
My heart would hear her and beat,
   Were it earth in an earthy bed;
My dust would hear her and beat,
   Had I lain for a century dead;
Would start and tremble under her feet,
   And blossom in purple and red.

XLIV

I

I HAVE led her home, my love, my only friend.
There is none like her, none.
And never yet so warmly ran my blood
And sweetly, on and on
Calming itself to the long-wish'd-for end,
Full to the banks, close on the promised good.

II

None like her, none.
Just now the dry-tongued laurels' pattering talk
Seem'd her light foot along the garden walk,
And shook my heart to think she comes once more;
But even then I heard her close the door,
The gates of Heaven are closed, and she is gone.

III

There is none like her, none.
Nor will be when our summers have deceased.
O, art thou sighing for Lebanon
In the long breeze that streams to thy delicious East,

Sighing for Lebanon,
Dark cedar, tho' thy limbs have here increased,
Upon a pastoral slope as fair,
And looking to the South, and fed
With honey'd rain and delicate air,
And haunted by the starry head
Of her whose gentle will has changed my fate,
And made my life a perfumed altar-flame;
And over whom thy darkness must have spread
With such delight as theirs of old, thy great
Forefathers of the thornless garden, there
Shadowing the snow-limb'd Eve from whom she came.

IV

Here will I lie, while these long branches sway,
And you fair stars that crown a happy day
Go in and out as if at merry play,
Who am no more so all forlorn,
As when it seem'd far better to be born
To labour and the mattock-harden'd hand,
Than nursed at ease and brought to understand
A sad astrology, the boundless plan
That makes you tyrants in your iron skies,
Innumerable, pitiless, passionless eyes,
Cold fires, yet with power to burn and brand
His nothingness into man.

V

But now shine on, and what care I,
Who in this stormy gulf have found a pearl
The countercharm of space and hollow sky,
And do accept my madness, and would die
To save from some slight shame one simple girl.

VI

Would die; for sullen-seeming Death may give
More life to Love than is or ever was
In our low world, where yet 'tis sweet to live.
Let no one ask me how it came to pass;

It seems that I am happy, that to me
A livelier emerald twinkles in the grass,
A purer sapphire melts into the sea.

VII

Not die; but live a life of truest breath,
And teach true life to fight with mortal wrongs.
O, why should Love, like men in drinking-songs,
Spice his fair banquet with the dust of death?
Make answer, Maud my bliss,
Maud made my Maud by that long loving kiss,
Life of my life, wilt thou not answer this?
'The dusky strand of Death inwoven here
With dear Love's tie, makes Love Himself more
    dear.'

VIII

Is that enchanted moan only the swell
Of the long waves that roll in yonder bay?
And hark the clock within, the silver knell
Of twelve sweet hours that past in bridal white,
And died to live, long as my pulses play;
But now by this my love has closed her sight
And given false death her hand, and stol'n away
To dreamful wastes where footless fancies dwell
Among the fragments of the golden day.
May nothing there her maiden grace affright!
Dear heart, I feel with thee the drowsy spell.
My bride to be, my evermore delight,
My own heart's heart, my ownest own, farewell;
It is but for a little space I go:
And ye meanwhile far over moor and fell
Beat to the noiseless music of the night!
Has our whole earth gone nearer to the glow
Of your soft splendours that you look so bright?
I have climb'd nearer out of lonely Hell.
Beat, happy stars, timing with things below,
Beat with my heart more blest than heart can tell,
Blest, but for some dark undercurrent woe
That seems to draw—but it shall not be so:
Let all be well, be well.

XLV

I

O THAT 'twere possible
After long grief and pain
To find the arms of my true love
Round me once again !

II

When I was wont to meet her
In the silent woody places
By the home that gave me birth,
We stood tranced in long embraces
Mixt with kisses sweeter sweeter
Than anything on earth.

III

A shadow flits before me,
Not thou, but like to thee :
Ah Christ, that it were possible
For one short hour to see
The souls we loved, that they might tell us
What and where they be.

IV

It leads me forth at evening,
It lightly winds and steals
In a cold white robe before me,
When all my spirit reels
At the shouts, the leagues of lights,
And the roaring of the wheels.

V

Half the night I waste in sighs,
Half in dreams I sorrow after
The delight of early skies ;
In a wakeful doze I sorrow

For the hand, the lips, the eyes,
For the meeting of the morrow,
The delight of happy laughter,
The delight of low replies.

VI

'Tis a morning pure and sweet,
And a dewy splendour falls
On the little flower that clings
To the turrets and the walls;
'Tis a morning pure and sweet,
And the light and shadow fleet;
She is walking in the meadow,
And the woodland echo rings;
In a moment we shall meet;
She is singing in the meadow
And the rivulet at her feet
Ripples on in light and shadow
To the ballad that she sings.

VII

Do I hear her sing as of old,
My bird with the shining head,
My own dove with the tender eye?
But there rings on a sudden a passionate cry,
There is some one dying or dead,
And a sullen thunder is roll'd;
For a tumult shakes the city,
And I wake, my dream is fled;
In the shuddering dawn, behold,
Without knowledge, without pity,
By the curtains of my bed
That abiding phantom cold.

VIII

Get thee hence, nor come again,
Mix not memory with doubt,
Pass, thou deathlike type of pain,
Pass and cease to move about!
'Tis the blot upon the brain
That *will* show itself without.

IX

Then I rise, the eavedrops fall,
And the yellow vapours choke
The great city sounding wide;
The day comes, a dull red ball
Wrapt in drifts of lurid smoke
On the misty river-tide.

X

Thro' the hubbub of the market
I steal, a wasted frame,
It crosses here, it crosses there,
Thro' all that crowd confused and loud,
The shadow still the same;
And on my heavy eyelids
My anguish hangs like shame.

XI

Alas for her that met me,
That heard me softly call,
Came glimmering thro' the laurels
At the quiet evenfall,
In the garden by the turrets
Of the old manorial hall.

XII

Would the happy spirit descend,
From the realms of light and song,
In the chamber or the street,
As she looks among the blest,
Should I fear to greet my friend
Or to say 'Forgive the wrong,'
Or to ask her, 'Take me, sweet,
To the regions of thy rest'?

XIII

But the broad light glares and beats,
And the shadow flits and fleets
And will not let me be;
And I loathe the squares and streets,

And the faces that one meets,
Hearts with no love for me:
Always I long to creep
Into some still cavern deep,
There to weep, and weep, and weep
My whole soul out to thee.

XLVI

Tears, idle tears, I know not what they mean,
Tears from the depth of some divine despair
Rise in the heart, and gather to the eyes,
In looking on the happy Autumn-fields,
And thinking of the days that are no more.

Fresh as the first beam glittering on a sail,
That brings our friends up from the underworld,
Sad as the last which reddens over one
That sinks with all we love below the verge;
So sad, so fresh, the days that are no more.

Ah, sad and strange as in dark summer dawns
The earliest pipe of half-awaken'd birds
To dying ears, when unto dying eyes
The casement slowly grows a glimmering square;
So sad, so strange, the days that are no more.

Dear as remember'd kisses after death,
And sweet as those by hopeless fancy feign'd
On lips that are for others; deep as love,
Deep as first love, and wild with all regret;
O Death in Life, the days that are no more.

XLVII

Late, late, so late! and dark the night and chill!
Late, late, so late! but we can enter still.
Too late, too late! ye cannot enter now.

No light had we: for that we do repent;
And learning this, the bridegroom will relent.
Too late, too late! ye cannot enter now.

No light : so late ! and dark and chill the night !
O let us in, that we may find the light !
Too late, too late : ye cannot enter now.

Have we not heard the bridegroom is so sweet ?
O let us in, tho' late, to kiss his feet !
No, no, too late ! ye cannot enter now.

XLVIII

TURN, Fortune, turn thy wheel and lower the proud ;
Turn thy wild wheel thro' sunshine, storm, and cloud ;
Thy wheel and thee we neither love nor hate.

Turn, Fortune, turn thy wheel with smile or frown ;
With that wild wheel we go not up or down ;
Our hoard is little, but our hearts are great.

Smile and we smile, the lords of many lands ;
Frown and we smile, the lords of our own hands ;
For man is man and master of his fate.

Turn, turn thy wheel above the staring crowd ;
Thy wheel and thou are shadows in the cloud ;
Thy wheel and thee we neither love nor hate.

XLIX

IN Love, if Love be Love, if Love be ours,
Faith and unfaith can ne'er be equal powers :
Unfaith in aught is want of faith in all.

It is the little rift within the lute,
That by and by will make the music mute,
And ever widening slowly silence all.

The little rift within the lover's lute
Or little pitted speck in garner'd fruit,
That rotting inward slowly moulders all.

It is not worth the keeping : let it go :
But shall it ? answer, darling, answer, no.
And trust me not at all or all in all.

I.

Sweet is true love tho' given in vain, in vain;
And sweet is death who puts an end to pain:
I know not which is sweeter, no, not I.

Love, art thou sweet? then bitter death must be:
Love, thou art bitter; sweet is death to me.
O Love, if death be sweeter, let me die.

Sweet love, that seems not made to fade away,
Sweet death, that seems to make us loveless clay,
I know not which is sweeter, no, not I.

I fain would follow love, if that could be;
I needs must follow death, who calls for me;
Call and I follow, I follow! let me die.

LI

MARIANA

'Mariana in the moated grange.'
Measure for Measure

With blackest moss the flower-plots
  Were thickly crusted, one and all:
The rusted nails fell from the knots
  That held the pear to the gable-wall.
The broken sheds look'd sad and strange:
  Unlifted was the clinking latch;
  Weeded and worn the ancient thatch
Upon the lonely moated grange.
      She only said, 'My life is dreary,
        He cometh not,' she said;
      She said, 'I am aweary, aweary,
        I would that I were dead!'

Her tears fell with the dews at even;
  Her tears fell ere the dews were dried;
She could not look on the sweet heaven,
  Either at morn or eventide.

After the flitting of the bats,
　When thickest dark did trance the sky,
　She drew her casement-curtain by,
And glanced athwart the glooming flats.
　　She only said, 'The night is dreary,
　　　He cometh not,' she said;
　　She said, 'I am aweary, aweary,
　　　I would that I were dead!'

Upon the middle of the night,
　Waking she heard the night-fowl crow:
The cock sung out an hour ere light:
　From the dark fen the oxen's low
Came to her: without hope of change,
　In sleep she seem'd to walk forlorn,
　Till cold winds woke the gray-eyed morn
About the lonely moated grange.
　　She only said, 'The day is dreary,
　　　He cometh not,' she said;
　　She said, 'I am aweary, aweary,
　　　I would that I were dead!'

About a stone-cast from the wall
　A sluice with blacken'd waters slept,
And o'er it many, round and small,
　The cluster'd marish-mosses crept.
Hard by a poplar shook alway,
　All silver-green with gnarled bark:
　For leagues no other tree did mark
The level waste, the rounding gray.
　　She only said, 'My life is dreary,
　　　He cometh not,' she said;
　　She said, 'I am aweary, aweary,
　　　I would that I were dead!'

And ever when the moon was low,
　And the shrill winds were up and away,
In the white curtain, to and fro,
　She saw the gusty shadow sway.
But when the moon was very low,
　And wild winds bound within their cell,
　The shadow of the poplar fell
Upon her bed, across her brow.

She only said, 'The night is dreary,
   He cometh not,' she said;
She said, 'I am aweary, aweary,
   I would that I were dead!'

All day within the dreamy house,
   The doors upon their hinges creak'd;
The blue fly sung in the pane; the mouse
   Behind the mouldering wainscot shriek'd,
Or from the crevice peer'd about.
   Old faces glimmer'd thro' the doors,
   Old footsteps trod the upper floors,
Old voices called her from without.
   She only said, 'My life is dreary,
      He cometh not,' she said;
   She said, 'I am aweary, aweary,
      I would that I were dead!'

The sparrow's chirrup on the roof,
   The slow clock ticking, and the sound
Which to the wooing wind aloof
   The poplar made, did all confound
Her sense; but most she loathed the hour
   When the thick-moted sunbeam lay
   Athwart the chambers, and the day
Was sloping toward his western bower.
   Then, said she, 'I am very dreary,
      He will not come,' she said;
   She wept, 'I am aweary, aweary,
      Oh God, that I were dead!'

LII

MARIANA IN THE SOUTH

WITH one black shadow at its feet,
   The house thro' all the level shines,
Close-latticed to the brooding heat,
   And silent in its dusty vines:

A faint-blue ridge upon the right,
　　An empty river-bed before,
　　And shallows on a distant shore,
In glaring sand and inlets bright.
　　　But 'Ave Mary,' made she moan,
　　　　And 'Ave Mary,' night and morn,
　　　And 'Ah,' she sang, 'to be all alone,
　　　　To live forgotten, and love forlorn.'

She, as her carol sadder grew,
　　From brow and bosom slowly down
Thro' rosy taper fingers drew
　　Her streaming curls of deepest brown
To left and right, and made appear
　　Still-lighted in a secret shrine,
　　Her melancholy eyes divine,
The home of woe without a tear.
　　　And 'Ave Mary,' was her moan,
　　　　'Madonna, sad is night and morn,'
　　　And 'Ah,' she sang, 'to be all alone,
　　　　To live forgotten, and love forlorn.'

Till all the crimson changed, and past
　　Into deep orange o'er the sea,
Low on her knees herself she cast,
　　Before Our Lady murmur'd she;
Complaining, 'Mother, give me grace
　　To help me of my weary load.'
　　And on the liquid mirror glow'd
The clear perfection of her face.
　　　'Is this the form,' she made her moan,
　　　　'That won his praises night and morn?'
　　　And 'Ah,' she said, 'but I wake alone,
　　　　I sleep forgotten, I wake forlorn.'

Nor bird would sing, nor lamb would bleat,
　　Nor any cloud would cross the vault,
But day increased from heat to heat,
　　On stony drought and steaming salt;
Till now at noon she slept again,
　　And seem'd knee-deep in mountain grass,
　　And heard her native breezes pass,
And runlets babbling down the glen.

She breathed in sleep a lower moan,
　　And murmuring, as at night and morn,
She thought, 'My spirit is here alone,
　　Walks forgotten, and is forlorn.'

Dreaming, she knew it was a dream :
　　She felt he was and was not there.
She woke : the babble of the stream
　　Fell, and, without, the steady glare
Shrank one sick willow sere and small.
　　The river-bed was dusty-white ;
　　And all the furnace of the light
Struck up against the blinding wall.
　　She whisper'd, with a stifled moan
　　　　More inward than at night or morn,
　　'Sweet Mother, let me not here alone
　　　　Live forgotten and die forlorn.'

And, rising, from her bosom drew
　　Old letters, breathing of her worth,
For 'Love,' they said, 'must needs be true,
　　To what is loveliest upon earth.'
An image seem'd to pass the door,
　　To look at her with slight, and say
　　'But now thy beauty flows away,
So be alone for evermore.'
　　　　'O cruel heart,' she changed her tone,
　　　　　　'And cruel love, whose end is scorn,
　　　　Is this the end to be left alone,
　　　　　　To live forgotten, and die forlorn ?'

But sometimes in the falling day
　　An image seem'd to pass the door,
To look into her eyes and say,
　　'But thou shalt be alone no more.'
And flaming downward over all
　　From heat to heat the day decreased,
　　And slowly rounded to the east
The one black shadow from the wall.
　　'The day to night,' she made her moan,
　　　　'The day to night, the night to morn,
　　And day and night I am left alone
　　　　To live forgotten, and love forlorn.'

At eve a dry cicala sung,
   There came a sound as of the sea;
Backward the lattice-blind she flung,
   And lean'd upon the balcony.
There all in spaces rosy-bright
   Large Hesper glitter'd on her tears,
   And deepening thro' the silent spheres
Heaven over Heaven rose the night.
And weeping then she made her moan,
   'The night comes on that knows not morn,
When I shall cease to be all alone,
   To live forgotten, and love forlorn.'

LIII
THE SISTERS

WE were two daughters of one race:
She was the fairest in the face:
   The wind is blowing in turret and tree.
They were together, and she fell;
Therefore revenge became me well.
   O the Earl was fair to see!

She died: she went to burning flame:
She mix'd her ancient blood with shame.
   The wind is howling in turret and tree.
Whole weeks and months, and early and late,
To win his love I lay in wait:
   O the Earl was fair to see!

I made a feast; I bad him come;
I won his love, I brought him home.
   The wind is roaring in turret and tree.
And after supper, on a bed,
Upon my lap he laid his head:
   O the Earl was fair to see!

I kiss'd his eyelids into rest:
His ruddy cheek upon my breast.

The wind is raging in turret and tree.
I hated him with the hate of hell,
But I loved his beauty passing well.
  O the Earl was fair to see !

I rose up in the silent night :
I made my dagger sharp and bright.
  The wind is raving in turret and tree.
As half-asleep his breath he drew,
Three times I stabb'd him thro' and thro'.
  O the Earl was fair to see !

I curl'd and comb'd his comely head,
He look'd so grand when he was dead.
  The wind is blowing in turret and tree.
I wrapt his body in the sheet,
And laid him at his mother's feet.
  O the Earl was fair to see !

LIV

THE LORD OF BURLEIGH

In her ear he whispers gaily,
  'If my heart by signs can tell,
Maiden, I have watch'd thee daily,
  And I think thou lov'st me well.'
She replies, in accents fainter,
  'There is none I love like thee.'
He is but a landscape-painter,
  And a village maiden she.
He to lips, that fondly falter,
  Presses his without reproof :
Leads her to the village altar,
  And they leave her father's roof.
'I can make no marriage present :
  Little can I give my wife.
Love will make our cottage pleasant,
  And I love thee more than life.'
They by parks and lodges going
  See the lordly castles stand :

Summer woods, about them blowing,
    Made a murmur in the land.
From deep thought himself he rouses,
    Says to her that loves him well,
'Let us see these handsome houses
    Where the wealthy nobles dwell.'
So she goes by him attended,
    Hears him lovingly converse,
Sees whatever fair and splendid
    Lay betwixt his home and hers;
Parks with oak and chestnut shady,
    Parks and order'd gardens great,
Ancient homes of lord and lady,
    Built for pleasure and for state.
All he shows her makes him dearer:
    Evermore she seems to gaze
On that cottage growing nearer,
    Where they twain will spend their days.
O but she will love him truly!
    He shall have a cheerful home;
She will order all things duly,
    When beneath his roof they come.
Thus her heart rejoices greatly,
    Till a gateway she discerns
With armorial bearings stately,
    And beneath the gate she turns;
Sees a mansion more majestic
    Than all those she saw before:
Many a gallant gay domestic
    Bows before him at the door.
And they speak in gentle murmur,
    When they answer to his call,
While he treads with footstep firmer,
    Leading on from hall to hall.
And, while now she wonders blindly,
    Nor the meaning can divine,
Proudly turns he round and kindly,
    'All of this is mine and thine.'
Here he lives in state and bounty,
    Lord of Burleigh, fair and free,
Not a lord in all the county
    Is so great a lord as he.

All at once the colour flushes
  Her sweet face from brow to chin:
As it were with shame she blushes,
  And her spirit changed within.
Then her countenance all over
  Pale again as death did prove:
But he clasp'd her like a lover,
  And he cheer'd her soul with love.
So she strove against her weakness,
  Tho' at times her spirit sank:
Shaped her heart with woman's meekness
  To all duties of her rank:
And a gentle consort made he,
  And her gentle mind was such
That she grew a noble lady,
  And the people loved her much.
But a trouble weigh'd upon her,
  And perplex'd her, night and morn,
With the burthen of an honour
  Unto which she was not born.
Faint she grew, and ever fainter,
  And she murmur'd, 'Oh, that he
Were once more that landscape-painter,
  Which did win my heart from me!'
So she droop'd and droop'd before him,
  Fading slowly from his side:
Three fair children first she bore him,
  Then before her time she died.
Weeping, weeping late and early,
  Walking up and pacing down,
Deeply mourn'd the Lord of Burleigh,
  Burleigh-house by Stamford-town.
And he came to look upon her,
  And he look'd at her and said,
'Bring the dress and put it on her,
  That she wore when she was wed.'
Then her people, softly treading,
  Bore to earth her body, drest
In the dress that she was wed in,
  That her spirit might have rest.

LV

LADY CLARA VERE DE VERE

Lady Clara Vere de Vere,
   Of me you shall not win renown:
You thought to break a country heart
   For pastime, ere you went to town.
At me you smiled, but unbeguiled
   I saw the snare, and I retired:
The daughter of a hundred Earls,
   You are not one to be desired.

Lady Clara Vere de Vere,
   I know you proud to bear your name,
Your pride is yet no mate for mine,
   Too proud to care from whence I came.
Nor would I break for your sweet sake
   A heart that doats on truer charms.
A simple maiden in her flower
   Is worth a hundred coats-of-arms.

Lady Clara Vere de Vere,
   Some meeker pupil you must find,
For were you queen of all that is,
   I could not stoop to such a mind.
You sought to prove how I could love,
   And my disdain is my reply.
The lion on your old stone gates
   Is not more cold to you than I.

Lady Clara Vere de Vere,
   You put strange memories in my head.
Not thrice your branching limes have blown
   Since I beheld young Laurence dead.
Oh your sweet eyes, your low replies:
   A great enchantress you may be;
But there was that across his throat
   Which you had hardly cared to see.

Lady Clara Vere de Vere,
   When thus he met his mother's view,
She had the passions of her kind,
   She spake some certain truths of you.
Indeed I heard one bitter word
   That scarce is fit for you to hear;
Her manners had not that repose
   Which stamps the caste of Vere de Vere.

Lady Clara Vere de Vere,
   There stands a spectre in your hall:
The guilt of blood is at your door:
   You changed a wholesome heart to gall.
You held your course without remorse,
   To make him trust his modest worth,
And, last, you fix'd a vacant stare,
   And slew him with your noble birth.

Trust me, Clara Vere de Vere,
   From yon blue heavens above us bent
The gardener Adam and his wife
   Smile at the claims of long descent.
Howe'er it be, it seems to me,
   'Tis only noble to be good.
Kind hearts are more than coronets,
   And simple faith than Norman blood.

I know you, Clara Vere de Vere,
   You pine among your halls and towers:
The languid light of your proud eyes
   Is wearied of the rolling hours.
In glowing health, with boundless wealth,
   But sickening of a vague disease,
You know so ill to deal with time,
   You needs must play such pranks as these.

Clara, Clara Vere de Vere,
   If time be heavy on your hands,
Are there no beggars at your gate,
   Nor any poor about your lands?
Oh! teach the orphan-boy to read,
   Or teach the orphan-girl to sew,
Pray Heaven for a human heart,
   And let the foolish yeoman go.

LVI

THE BEGGAR MAID

HER arms across her breast she laid;
    She was more fair than words can say:
Bare-footed came the beggar maid
    Before the king Cophetua.
In robe and crown the king stept down,
    To meet and greet her on her way;
'It is no wonder,' said the lords,
    'She is more beautiful than day.'

As shines the moon in clouded skies,
    She in her poor attire was seen:
One praised her ancles, one her eyes,
    One her dark hair and lovesome mien.
So sweet a face, such angel grace,
    In all that land had never been:
Cophetua sware a royal oath:
    'This beggar maid shall be my queen!'

LVII

THE TALKING OAK

ONCE more the gate behind me falls;
    Once more before my face
I see the moulder'd Abbey-walls,
    That stand within the chace.

Beyond the lodge the city lies,
    Beneath its drift of smoke;
And ah! with what delighted eyes
    I turn to yonder oak.

For when my passion first began,
    Ere that, which in me burn'd,
The love, that makes me thrice a man,
    Could hope itself return'd;

To yonder oak within the field
   I spoke without restraint,
And with a larger faith appeal'd
   Than Papist unto Saint.

For oft I talk'd with him apart,
   And told him of my choice,
Until he plagiarised a heart,
   And answer'd with a voice.

Tho' what he whisper'd under Heaven
   None else could understand;
I found him garrulously given,
   A babbler in the land.

But since I heard him make reply
   Is many a weary hour;
'Twere well to question him, and try
   If yet he keeps the power.

Hail, hidden to the knees in fern,
   Broad Oak of Sumner-chace,
Whose topmost branches can discern
   The roofs of Sumner-place!

Say thou, whereon I carved her name,
   If ever maid or spouse,
As fair as my Olivia, came
   To rest beneath thy boughs.—

'O Walter, I have shelter'd here
   Whatever maiden grace
The good old Summers, year by year
   Made ripe in Sumner-chace:

'Old Summers, when the monk was fat,
   And, issuing shorn and sleek,
Would twist his girdle tight, and pat
   The girls upon the cheek,

'Ere yet, in scorn of Peter's-pence,
   And number'd bead, and shrift,
Bluff Harry broke into the spence
   And turn'd the cowls adrift:

' And I have seen some score of those
    Fresh faces, that would thrive
When his man-minded offset rose
    To chase the deer at five;

' And all that from the town would stroll,
    Till that wild wind made work
In which the gloomy brewer's soul
    Went by me, like a stork:

' The slight she-slips of loyal blood,
    And others, passing praise,
Strait-laced, but all-too-full in bud
    For puritanic stays:

' And I have shadow'd many a group
    Of beauties, that were born
In teacup-times of hood and hoop,
    Or while the patch was worn;

' And, leg and arm with love-knots gay,
    About me leap'd and laugh'd
The modish Cupid of the day,
    And shrill'd his tinsel shaft.

' I swear (and else may insects prick
    Each leaf into a gall)
This girl, for whom your heart is sick,
    Is three times worth them all;

' For those and theirs, by Nature's law,
    Have faded long ago;
But in these latter springs I saw
    Your own Olivia blow,

' From when she gamboll'd on the greens
    A baby-germ, to when
The maiden blossoms of her teens
    Could number five from ten.

' I swear, by leaf, and wind, and rain,
    (And hear me with thine ears,)
That, tho' I circle in the grain
    Five hundred rings of years—

The Talking Oak

'Yet, since I first could cast a shade,
   Did never creature pass
So slightly, musically made,
   So light upon the grass:

'For as to fairies, that will flit
   To make the greensward fresh,
I hold them exquisitely knit,
   But far too spare of flesh.'

Oh, hide thy knotted knees in fern,
   And overlook the chace;
And from thy topmost branch discern
   The roofs of Sumner-place.

But thou, whereon I carved her name,
   That oft hast heard my vows,
Declare when last Olivia came
   To sport beneath thy boughs.

'O yesterday, you know, the fair
   Was holden at the town;
Her father left his good arm-chair,
   And rode his hunter down.

'And with him Albert came on his
   I look'd at him with joy:
As cowslip unto oxlip is,
   So seems she to the boy.

'An hour had past—and, sitting straight
   Within the low-wheel'd chaise,
Her mother trundled to the gate
   Behind the dappled grays.

'But as for her, she stay'd at home,
   And on the roof she went,
And down the way you use to come,
   She look'd with discontent.

'She left the novel half-uncut
   Upon the rosewood shelf;
She left the new piano shut:
   She could not please herself.

'Then ran she, gamesome as the colt,
    And livelier than a lark
She sent her voice thro' all the holt
    Before her, and the park.

'A light wind chased her on the wing,
    And in the chase grew wild,
As close as might be would he cling
    About the darling child:

'But light as any wind that blows
    So fleetly did she stir,
The flower, she touch'd on, dipt and rose,
    And turn'd to look at her.

'And here she came, and round me play'd,
    And sang to me the whole
Of those three stanzas that you made
    About my "giant bole;"

'And in a fit of frolic mirth
    She strove to span my waist:
Alas, I was so broad of girth,
    I could not be embraced.

'I wish'd myself the fair young beech
    That here beside me stands,
That round me, clasping each in each,
    She might have lock'd her hands.

'Yet seem'd the pressure thrice as sweet
    As woodbine's fragile hold,
Or when I feel about my feet
    The berried briony fold.'

O muffle round thy knees with fern,
    And shadow Sumner-chace!
Long may thy topmost branch discern
    The roofs of Sumner-place!

But tell me, did she read the name
    I carved with many vows
When last with throbbing heart I came
    To rest beneath thy boughs?

The Talking Oak

'O yes, she wander'd round and round
    These knotted knees of mine,
And found, and kiss'd the name she found,
    And sweetly murmur'd thine.

'A teardrop trembled from its source,
    And down my surface crept.
My sense of touch is something coarse,
    But I believe she wept.

'Then flush'd her cheek with rosy light,
    She glanced across the plain;
But not a creature was in sight:
    She kiss'd me once again.

'Her kisses were so close and kind,
    That, trust me on my word,
Hard wood I am, and wrinkled rind,
    But yet my sap was stirr'd:

'And even into my inmost ring
    A pleasure I discern'd,
Like those blind motions of the Spring,
    That show the year is turn'd.

'Thrice-happy he that may caress
    The ringlet's waving balm—
The cushions of whose touch may press
    The maiden's tender palm.

'I, rooted here among the groves
    But languidly adjust
My vapid vegetable loves
    With anthers and with dust:

'For ah! my friend, the days were brief
    Whereof the poets talk,
When that, which breathes within the leaf,
    Could slip its bark and walk.

'But could I, as in times foregone,
    From spray, and branch, and stem,
Have suck'd and gather'd into one
    The life that spreads in them,

'She had not found me so remiss;
   But lightly issuing thro',
I would have paid her kiss for kiss,
   With usury thereto.'

O flourish high, with leafy towers,
   And overlook the lea,
Pursue thy loves among the bowers
   But leave thou mine to me.

O flourish, hidden deep in fern,
   Old oak, I love thee well;
A thousand thanks for what I learn
   And what remains to tell.

' 'Tis little more: the day was warm;
   At last, tired out with play,
She sank her head upon her arm
   And at my feet she lay.

' Her eyelids dropp'd their silken eaves.
   I breathed upon her eyes
Thro' all the summer of my leaves
   A welcome mix'd with sighs.

' I took the swarming sound of life—
   The music from the town—
The murmurs of the drum and fife
   And lull'd them in my own.

' Sometimes I let a sunbeam slip,
   To light her shaded eye;
A second flutter'd round her lip
   Like a golden butterfly;

' A third would glimmer on her neck
   To make the necklace shine;
Another slid, a sunny fleck,
   From head to ancle fine,

' Then close and dark my arms I spread,
   And shadow'd all her rest—
Dropt dews upon her golden head,
   An acorn in her breast.

'But in a pet she started up,
    And pluck'd it out, and drew
My little oakling from the cup,
    And flung him in the dew.

'And yet it was a graceful gift—
    I felt a pang within
As when I see the woodman lift
    His axe to slay my kin.

'I shook him down because he was
    The finest on the tree.
He lies beside thee on the grass.
    O kiss him once for me.

'O kiss him twice and thrice for me,
    That have no lips to kiss,
For never yet was oak on lea
    Shall grow so fair as this.'

Step deeper yet in herb and fern,
    Look further thro' the chace,
Spread upward till thy boughs discern
    The front of Sumner-place.

This fruit of thine by Love is blest,
    That but a moment lay
Where fairer fruit of Love may rest
    Some happy future day.

I kiss it twice, I kiss it thrice,
    The warmth it thence shall win
To riper life may magnetise
    The baby-oak within.

But thou, while kingdoms overset,
    Or lapse from hand to hand,
Thy leaf shall never fail, nor yet
    Thine acorn in the land.

May never saw dismember thee,
    Nor wielded axe disjoint,
Thou art the fairest-spoken tree
    From here to Lizard-point.

The Talking Oak

O rock upon thy towery-top
    All throats that gurgle sweet!
All starry culmination drop
    Balm-dews to bathe thy feet!

All grass of silky feather grow—
    And while he sinks or swells
The full south-breeze around thee blow
    The sound of minster bells.

The fat earth feed thy branchy root,
    That under deeply strikes!
The northern morning o'er thee shoot,
    High up, in silver spikes!

Nor ever lightning char thy grain,
    But, rolling as in sleep,
Low thunders bring the mellow rain,
    That makes thee broad and deep!

And hear me swear a solemn oath,
    That only by thy side
Will I to Olive plight my troth,
    And gain her for my bride.

And when my marriage morn may fall,
    She, Dryad-like, shall wear
Alternate leaf and acorn-ball
    In wreath about her hair.

And I will work in prose and rhyme,
    And praise thee more in both
Than bard has honour'd beech or lime,
    Or that Thessalian growth,

In which the swarthy ringdove sat,
    And mystic sentence spoke;
And more than England honours that,
    Thy famous brother-oak,

Wherein the younger Charles abode
    Till all the paths were dim,
And far below the Roundhead rode,
    And humm'd a surly hymn.

LVIII

MILKMAID'S SONG

SHAME upon you, Robin,
    Shame upon you now!
Kiss me would you? with my hands
    Milking the cow?
    Daisies grow again,
    Kingcups blow again,
And you came and kiss'd me milking the cow.

Robin came behind me,
    Kiss'd me well I vow;
Cuff him could I? with my hands
    Milking the cow?
    Swallows fly again,
    Cuckoos cry again,
And you came and kiss'd me milking the cow.

Come, Robin, Robin,
    Come and kiss me now;
Help it can I? with my hands
    Milking the cow?
    Ringdoves coo again,
    All things woo again.
Come behind and kiss me milking the cow!

LIX

THE MILLER'S DAUGHTER

I SEE the wealthy miller yet,
    His double chin, his portly size,
And who that knew him could forget
    The busy wrinkles round his eyes?
The slow wise smile that, round about
    His dusty forehead drily curl'd,
Seem'd half-within and half-without,
    And full of dealings with the world?

In yonder chair I see him sit,
    Three fingers round the old silver cup—
I see his gray eyes twinkle yet
    At his own jest—gray eyes lit up
With summer lightnings of a soul
    So full of summer warmth, so glad,
So healthy, sound, and clear and whole,
    His memory scarce can make me sad.

Yet fill my glass: give me one kiss:
    My own sweet Alice, we must die.
There's somewhat in this world amiss
    Shall be unriddled by and by.
There's somewhat flows to us in life,
    But more is taken quite away.
Pray, Alice, pray, my darling wife,
    That we may die the self-same day.

Have I not found a happy earth?
    I least should breathe a thought of pain.
Would God renew me from my birth
    I'd almost live my life again.
So sweet it seems with thee to walk,
    And once again to woo thee mine—
It seems in after-dinner talk
    Across the walnuts and the wine—

To be the long and listless boy
    Late-left an orphan of the squire,
Where this old mansion mounted high
    Looks down upon the village spire:
For even here, where I and you
    Have lived and loved alone so long,
Each morn my sleep was broken thro'
    By some wild skylark's matin song.

And oft I heard the tender dove
    In firry woodlands making moan;
But ere I saw your eyes, my love,
    I had no motion of my own.
For scarce my life with fancy play'd
    Before I dream'd that pleasant dream—
Still hither thither idly sway'd
    Like those long mosses in the stream.

The Miller's Daughter

Or from the bridge I lean'd to hear
    The milldam rushing down with noise,
And see the minnows everywhere
    In crystal eddies glance and poise,
The tall flag-flowers when they sprung
    Below the range of stepping-stones,
Or those three chestnuts near, that hung
    In masses thick with milky cones.

But, Alice, what an hour was that,
    When after roving in the woods
('Twas April then), I came and sat
    Below the chestnuts, when their buds
Were glistening to the breezy blue;
    And on the slope, an absent fool,
I cast me down, nor thought of you,
    But angled in the higher pool.

A love-song I had somewhere read,
    An echo from a measured strain,
Beat time to nothing in my head
    From some odd corner of the brain.
It haunted me, the morning long,
    With weary sameness in the rhymes,
The phantom of a silent song,
    That went and came a thousand times.

Then leapt a trout. In lazy mood
    I watch'd the little circles die;
They past into the level flood,
    And there a vision caught my eye;
The reflex of a beauteous form,
    A glowing arm, a gleaming neck,
As when a sunbeam wavers warm
    Within the dark and dimpled beck.

For you remember, you had set,
    That morning, on the casement-edge
A long green box of mignonette,
    And you were leaning from the ledge:
And when I raised my eyes, above
    They met with two so full and bright—
Such eyes! I swear to you, my love,
    That these have never lost their light.

I loved, and love dispell'd the fear
    That I should die an early death:
For love possess'd the atmosphere,
    And fill'd the breast with purer breath.
My mother thought, What ails the boy?
    For I was alter'd, and began
To move about the house with joy,
    And with the certain step of man.

I loved the brimming wave that swam
    Thro' quiet meadows round the mill,
The sleepy pool above the dam,
    The pool beneath it never still,
The meal-sacks on the whiten'd floor,
    The dark round of the dripping wheel,
The very air about the door
    Made misty with the floating meal.

And oft in ramblings on the wold,
    When April nights began to blow,
And April's crescent glimmer'd cold,
    I saw the village lights below;
I knew your taper far away,
    And full at heart of trembling hope,
From off the wold I came, and lay
    Upon the freshly-flower'd slope.

The deep brook groan'd beneath the mill;
    And 'by that lamp,' I thought, 'she sits!'
The white chalk-quarry from the hill
    Gleam'd to the flying moon by fits.
'O that I were beside her now!
    O will she answer if I call?
O would she give me vow for vow,
    Sweet Alice, if I told her all?'

Sometimes I saw you sit and spin;
    And, in the pauses of the wind,
Sometimes I heard you sing within;
    Sometimes your shadow cross'd the blind.
At last you rose and moved the light,
    And the long shadow of the chair
Flitted across into the night,
    And all the casement darken'd there.

But when at last I dared to speak,
   The lanes, you know, were white with may,
Your ripe lips moved not, but your cheek
   Flush'd like the coming of the day;
And so it was—half-sly, half-shy,
   You would, and would not, little one!
Although I pleaded tenderly,
   And you and I were all alone.

And slowly was my mother brought
   To yield consent to my desire:
She wish'd me happy, but she thought
   I might have look'd a little higher;
And I was young—too young to wed:
   'Yet must I love her for your sake;
Go fetch your Alice here,' she said:
   Her eyelid quiver'd as she spake.

And down I went to fetch my bride:
   But, Alice, you were ill at ease;
This dress and that by turns you tried,
   Too fearful that you should not please.
I loved you better for your fears,
   I knew you could not look but well;
And dews, that would have fall'n in tears,
   I kiss'd away before they fell.

I watch'd the little flutterings,
   The doubt my mother would not see;
She spoke at large of many things,
   And at the last she spoke of me;
And turning look'd upon your face,
   As near this door you sat apart,
And rose, and, with a silent grace
   Approaching, press'd you heart to heart.

Ah, well—but sing the foolish song
   I gave you, Alice, on the day
When, arm in arm, we went along,
   A pensive pair, and you were gay
With bridal flowers—that I may seem,
   As in the nights of old, to lie
Beside the mill-wheel in the stream,
   While those full chestnuts whisper by.

It is the miller's daughter,
  And she is grown so dear, so dear,
That I would be the jewel
  That trembles in her ear:
For hid in ringlets day and night,
I'd touch her neck so warm and white.

And I would be the girdle
  About her dainty dainty waist,
And her heart would beat against me,
  In sorrow and in rest:
And I should know if it beat right,
I'd clasp it round so close and tight.

And I would be the necklace,
  And all day long to fall and rise
Upon her balmy bosom,
  With her laughter or her sighs,
And I would lie so light, so light,
I scarce should be unclasp'd at night.

A trifle, sweet! which true love spells—
  True love interprets—right alone.
His light upon the letter dwells,
  For all the spirit is his own.
So, if I waste words now, in truth
  You must blame Love. His early rage
Had force to make me rhyme in youth,
  And makes me talk too much in age.

And now those vivid hours are gone,
  Like mine own life to me thou art,
Where Past and Present, wound in one,
  Do make a garland for the heart:
So sing that other song I made,
  Half-anger'd with my happy lot,
The day, when in the chestnut shade
  I found the blue Forget-me-not.

> Love that hath us in the net,
> Can he pass, and we forget?
> Many suns arise and set.
> Many a chance the years beget.
> Love the gift is Love the debt.
>   Even so.

Love is hurt with jar and fret.
Love is made a vague regret.
Eyes with idle tears are wet.
Idle habit links us yet.
What is love? for we forget:
   Ah, no! no!

Look thro' mine eyes with thine.   True wife,
  Round my true heart thine arms entwine
My other dearer life in life,
  Look thro' my very soul with thine!
Untouch'd with any shade of years,
  May those kind eyes for ever dwell!
They have not shed a many tears,
  Dear eyes, since first I knew them well.

Yet tears they shed: they had their part
  Of sorrow: for when time was ripe,
The still affection of the heart
  Became an outward breathing type,
That into stillness past again,
  And left a want unknown before;
Although the loss had brought us pain,
  That loss but made us love the more,

With farther lookings on.   The kiss,
  The woven arms, seem but to be
Weak symbols of the settled bliss,
  The comfort, I have found in thee:
But that God bless thee, dear—who wrought
  Two spirits to one equal mind—
With blessings beyond hope or thought,
  With blessings which no words can find.

Arise, and let us wander forth,
  To yon old mill across the wolds;
For look, the sunset, south and north,
  Winds all the vale in rosy folds,
And fires your narrow casement glass,
  Touching the sullen pool below:
On the chalk-hill the bearded grass
  Is dry and dewless.   Let us go.

LX
THE LETTERS

I

STILL on the tower stood the vane,
   A black yew gloom'd the stagnant air,
I peer'd athwart the chancel pane
   And saw the altar cold and bare.
A clog of lead was round my feet,
   A band of pain across my brow;
'Cold altar, Heaven and earth shall meet
   Before you hear my marriage vow.'

II

I turn'd and humm'd a bitter song
   That mock'd the wholesome human heart,
And then we met in wrath and wrong,
   We met, but only meant to part.
Full cold my greeting was and dry;
   She faintly smiled, she hardly moved;
I saw with half-unconscious eye
   She wore the colours I approved.

III

She took the little ivory chest,
   With half a sigh she turn'd the key,
Then raised her head with lips comprest,
   And gave my letters back to me.
And gave the trinkets and the rings,
   My gifts, when gifts of mine could please;
As looks a father on the things
   Of his dead son, I look'd on these.

IV

She told me all her friends had said;
   I raged against the public liar;
She talk'd as if her love were dead,
   But in my words were seeds of fire.

'No more of love; your sex is known:
　　I never will be twice deceived.
Henceforth I trust the man alone,
　　The woman cannot be believed.

V

'Thro' slander, meanest spawn of Hell—
　　And women's slander is the worst,
And you, whom once I lov'd so well,
　　Thro' you, my life will be accurst.'
I spoke with heart, and heat and force,
　　I shook her breast with vague alarms—
Like torrents from a mountain source
　　We rush'd into each other's arms.

VI

We parted: sweetly gleam'd the stars,
　　And sweet the vapour-braided blue,
Low breezes fann'd the belfry bars,
　　As homeward by the church I drew.
The very graves appear'd to smile,
　　So fresh they rose in shadow'd swells;
'Dark porch,' I said, 'and silent aisle,
　　There comes a sound of marriage bells.'

LXI

TO J. S.

THE wind, that beats the mountain, blows
　　More softly round the open wold,
And gently comes the world to those
　　That are cast in gentle mould.

And me this knowledge bolder made,
　　Or else I had not dared to flow
In these words toward you, and invade
　　Even with a verse your holy woe.

To J. S.

'Tis strange that those we lean on most,
    Those in whose laps our limbs are nursed,
Fall into shadow, soonest lost:
    Those we love first are taken first.

God gives us love. Something to love
    He lends us; but, when love is grown
To ripeness, that on which it throve
    Falls off, and love is left alone.

This is the curse of time. Alas!
    In grief I am not all unlearn'd;
Once thro' mine own doors Death did pass;
    One went, who never hath return'd.

He will not smile—not speak to me
    Once more. Two years his chair is seen
Empty before us. That was he
    Without whose life I had not been.

Your loss is rarer; for this star
    Rose with you thro' a little arc
Of heaven, nor having wander'd far
    Shot on the sudden into dark.

I knew your brother: his mute dust
    I honour and his living worth:
A man more pure and bold and just
    Was never born into the earth

I have not look'd upon you nigh,
    Since that dear soul hath fall'n asleep.
Great Nature is more wise than I:
    I will not tell you not to weep.

And tho' mine own eyes fill with dew,
    Drawn from the spirit thro' the brain,
I will not even preach to you,
    'Weep, weeping dulls the inward pain.'

Let Grief be her own mistress still.
    She loveth her own anguish deep
More than much pleasure. Let her will
    Be done—to weep or not to weep.

To J. S.

I will not say, 'God's ordinance
    Of Death is blown in every wind;'
For that is not a common chance
    That takes away a noble mind.

His memory long will live alone
    In all our hearts, as mournful light
That broods above the fallen sun,
    And dwells in heaven half the night.

Vain solace! Memory standing near
    Cast down her eyes, and in her throat
Her voice seem'd distant, and a tear
    Dropt on the letters as I wrote.

I wrote I know not what. In truth,
    How *should* I soothe you anyway,
Who miss the brother of your youth?
    Yet something I did wish to say:

For he too was a friend to me:
    Both are my friends, and my true breast
Bleedeth for both; yet it may be
    That only silence suiteth best.

Words weaker than your grief would make
    Grief more. 'Twere better I should cease
Although myself could almost take
    The place of him that sleeps in peace.

Sleep sweetly, tender heart, in peace:
    Sleep, holy spirit, blessed soul,
While the stars burn, the moons increase,
    And the great ages onward roll.

Sleep till the end, true soul and sweet.
    Nothing comes to thee new or strange.
Sleep full of rest from head to feet;
    Lie still, dry dust, secure of change.

LXII

You ask me, why, tho' ill at ease,
    Within this region I subsist,
    Whose spirits falter in the mist,
And languish for the purple seas.

It is the land that freemen till,
    That sober-suited Freedom chose,
    The land, where girt with friends or foes
A man may speak the thing he will;

A land of settled government,
    A land of just and old renown,
    Where Freedom slowly broadens down
From precedent to precedent:

Where faction seldom gathers head,
    But by degrees to fulness wrought,
    The strength of some diffusive thought
Hath time and space to work and spread.

Should banded unions persecute
    Opinion, and induce a time
    When single thought is civil crime,
And individual freedom mute;

Tho' Power should make from land to land
    The name of Britain trebly great—
    Tho' every channel of the State
Should fill and choke with golden sand—

Yet waft me from the harbour-mouth,
    Wild wind! I seek a warmer sky,
    And I will see before I die
The palms and temples of the South.

LXIII

Of old sat Freedom on the heights,
    The thunders breaking at her feet:
Above her shook the starry lights:
    She heard the torrents meet.

There in her place she did rejoice,
    Self-gather'd in her prophet-mind,
But fragments of her mighty voice
    Came rolling on the wind.

Then stept she down thro' town and field
    To mingle with the human race,
And part by part to men reveal'd
    The fulness of her face—

Grave mother of majestic works,
    From her isle-altar gazing down,
Who, God-like, grasps the triple forks,
    And, King-like, wears the crown:

Her open eyes desire the truth.
    The wisdom of a thousand years
Is in them. May perpetual youth
    Keep dry their light from tears;

That her fair form may stand and shine,
    Make bright our days and light our dreams,
Turning to scorn with lips divine
    The falsehood of extremes!

LXIV

LOVE thou thy land, with love far-brought
    From out the storied Past, and used
    Within the Present, but transfused
Thro' future time by power of thought.

True love turn'd round on fixed poles,
    Love, that endures not sordid ends,
    For English natures, freemen, friends,
Thy brothers and immortal souls.

But pamper not a hasty time,
    Nor feed with crude imaginings
    The herd, wild hearts and feeble wings
That every sophister can lime.

Deliver not the tasks of might
   To weakness, neither hide the ray
   From those, not blind, who wait for day,
Tho' sitting girt with doubtful light.

Make knowledge circle with the winds;
   But let her herald, Reverence, fly
   Before her to whatever sky
Bear seed of men and growth of minds.

Watch what main-currents draw the years:
   Cut Prejudice against the grain:
   But gentle words are always gain:
Regard the weakness of thy peers:

Nor toil for title, place, or touch
   Of pension, neither count on praise:
   It grows to guerdon after-days:
Nor deal in watch-words overmuch:

Not clinging to some ancient saw;
   Not master'd by some modern term;
   Not swift nor slow to change, but firm:
And in its season bring the law;

That from Discussion's lip may fall
   With Life, that, working strongly, binds—
   Set in all lights by many minds,
To close the interests of all.

For Nature also, cold and warm,
   And moist and dry, devising long,
   Thro' many agents making strong,
Matures the individual form.

Meet is it changes should control
   Our being, lest we rust in ease.
   We all are changed by still degrees,
All but the basis of the soul.

So let the change which comes be free
   To ingroove itself with that which flies,
   And work, a joint of state, that plies
Its office, moved with sympathy.

A saying, hard to shape in act;
  For all the past of Time reveals
  A bridal dawn of thunder-peals,
Wherever Thought hath wedded Fact.

Ev'n now we hear with inward strife
  A motion toiling in the gloom—
  The Spirit of the years to come
Yearning to mix himself with Life.

A slow-develop'd strength awaits
  Completion in a painful school;
  Phantoms of other forms of rule,
New Majesties of mighty States—

The warders of the growing hour,
  But vague in vapour, hard to mark;
  And round them sea and air are dark
With great contrivances of Power.

Of many changes, aptly join'd,
  Is bodied forth the second whole.
  Regard gradation, lest the soul
Of Discord race the rising wind;

A wind to puff your idol-fires,
  And heap their ashes on the head;
  To shame the boast so often made,
That we are wiser than our sires.

Oh yet, if Nature's evil star
  Drive men in manhood, as in youth,
  To follow flying steps of Truth
Across the brazen bridge of war—

If New and Old, disastrous feud,
  Must ever shock, like armed foes,
  And this be true, till Time shall close,
That Principles are rain'd in blood;

Not yet the wise of heart would cease
  To hold his hope thro' shame and guilt,
  But with his hand against the hilt,
Would pace the troubled land, like Peace;

O

Not less, tho' dogs of Faction bay,
   Would serve his kind in deed and word,
   Certain, if knowledge bring the sword,
That knowledge takes the sword away—

Would love the gleams of good that broke
   From either side, nor veil his eyes:
   And if some dreadful need should rise
Would strike, and firmly, and one stroke:

To-morrow yet would reap to-day,
   As we bear blossom of the dead;
   Earn well the thrifty months, nor wed
Raw Haste, half-sister to Delay.

LXV

THE REVENGE

A BALLAD OF THE FLEET

I

At Flores in the Azores Sir Richard Grenville lay,
And a pinnace, like a flutter'd bird, came flying from far away:
'Spanish ships of war at sea! we have sighted fifty-three!'
Then sware Lord Thomas Howard: ''Fore God I am no coward;
But I cannot meet them here, for my ships are out of gear,
And the half my men are sick. I must fly, but follow quick.
We are six ships of the line; can we fight with fifty-three?'

II

Then spake Sir Richard Grenville: 'I know you are no coward;
You fly them for a moment to fight with them again.

But I've ninety men and more that are lying sick ashore.
I should count myself the coward if I left them, my Lord Howard,
To these Inquisition dogs and the devildoms of Spain.'

III

So Lord Howard past away with five ships of war that day,
Till he melted like a cloud in the silent summer heaven;
But Sir Richard bore in hand all his sick men from the land
Very carefully and slow,
Men of Bideford in Devon,
And we laid them on the ballast down below;
For we brought them all aboard,
And they blest him in their pain, that they were not left to Spain,
To the thumbscrew and the stake, for the glory of the Lord.

IV

He had only a hundred seamen to work the ship and to fight,
And he sailed away from Flores till the Spaniard came in sight,
With his huge sea-castles heaving upon the weather bow.
'Shall we fight or shall we fly?
Good Sir Richard, tell us now,
For to fight is but to die!
There'll be little of us left by the time this sun be set.'
And Sir Richard said again: 'We be all good English men.
Let us bang these dogs of Seville, the children of the devil,
For I never turn'd my back upon Don or devil yet.'

V

Sir Richard spoke and he laugh'd, and we roar'd a hurrah, and so
The little Revenge ran on sheer into the heart of the foe,
With her hundred fighters on deck, and her ninety sick below;
For half of their fleet to the right and half to the left were seen,
And the little Revenge ran on thro' the long sea-lane between.

VI

Thousands of their soldiers look'd down from their decks and laugh'd,
Thousands of their seamen made mock at the mad little craft
Running on and on, till delay'd
By their mountain-like San Philip that, of fifteen hundred tons,
And up-shadowing high above us with her yawning tiers of guns,
Took the breath from our sails, and we stay'd.

VII

And while now the great San Philip hung above us like a cloud
Whence the thunderbolt will fall
Long and loud,
Four galleons drew away
From the Spanish fleet that day,
And two upon the larboard and two upon the starboard lay,
And the battle-thunder broke from them all.

VIII

But anon the great San Philip, she bethought herself and went
Having that within her womb that had left her ill content;

And the rest they came aboard us, and they fought us hand to hand,
For a dozen times they came with their pikes and musqueteers,
And a dozen times we shook 'em off as a dog that shakes his ears
When he leaps from the water to the land.

IX

And the sun went down, and the stars came out far over the summer sea,
But never a moment ceased the fight of the one and the fifty-three.
Ship after ship, the whole night long, their high-built galleons came,
Ship after ship, the whole night long, with her battle-thunder and flame;
Ship after ship, the whole night long, drew back with her dead and her shame.
For some were sunk and many were shatter'd, and so could fight us no more—
God of battles, was ever a battle like this in the world before?

X

For he said 'Fight on! fight on!'
Tho' his vessel was all but a wreck;
And it chanced that, when half of the short summer night was gone,
With a grisly wound to be drest he had left the deck,
But a bullet struck him that was dressing it suddenly dead,
And himself he was wounded again in the side and the head,
And he said 'Fight on! fight on!'

XI

And the night went down, and the sun smiled out far over the summer sea,
And the Spanish fleet with broken sides lay round us all in a ring;

But they dared not touch us again, for they fear'd that we still could sting,
So they watch'd what the end would be.
And we had not fought them in vain,
But in perilous plight were we,
Seeing forty of our poor hundred were slain,
And half of the rest of us maim'd for life
In the crash of the cannonades and the desperate strife;
And the sick men down in the hold were most of them stark and cold,
And the pikes were all broken or bent, and the powder was all of it spent;
And the masts and the rigging were lying over the side;
But Sir Richard cried in his English pride,
'We have fought such a fight for a day and a night
As may never be fought again!
We have won great glory, my men!
And a day less or more
At sea or ashore,
We die—does it matter when?
Sink me the ship, Master Gunner—sink her, split her in twain!
Fall into the hands of God, not into the hands of Spain!'

XII

And the gunner said 'Ay, ay,' but the seamen made reply:
'We have children, we have wives,
And the Lord hath spared our lives.
We will make the Spaniard promise, if we yield, to let us go;
We shall live to fight again and to strike another blow.'
And the lion there lay dying, and they yielded to the foe.

XIII

And the stately Spanish men to their flagship bore him then,
Where they laid him by the mast, old Sir Richard caught at last,

And they praised him to his face with their courtly
    foreign grace;
But he rose upon their decks, and he cried:
'I have fought for Queen and Faith like a valiant man
    and true;
I have only done my duty as a man is bound to do:
With a joyful spirit I Sir Richard Grenville die!'
And he fell upon their decks, and he died.

XIV

And they stared at the dead that had been so valiant
    and true,
And had holden the power and glory of Spain so
    cheap
That he dared her with one little ship and his English
    few;
Was he devil or man? He was devil for aught they
    knew,
But they sank his body with honour down into the
    deep,
And they mann'd the Revenge with a swarthier alien
    crew,
And away she sail'd with her loss and long'd for her
    own;
When a wind from the lands they had ruin'd awoke
    from sleep,
And the water began to heave and the weather to
    moan,
And or ever that evening ended a great gale blew,
And a wave like the wave that is raised by an earth-
    quake grew,
Till it smote on their hulls and their sails and their
    masts and their flags,
And the whole sea plunged and fell on the shot-
    shatter'd navy of Spain,
And the little Revenge herself went down by the
    island crags
To be lost evermore in the main.

LXVI

ODE ON THE DEATH OF THE DUKE OF WELLINGTON

I

Bury the Great Duke
  With an empire's lamentation,
Let us bury the Great Duke
  To the noise of the mourning of a mighty nation,
Mourning when their leaders fall,
Warriors carry the warrior's pall,
And sorrow darkens hamlet and hall.

II

Where shall we lay the man whom we deplore?
Here, in streaming London's central roar.
Let the sound of those he wrought for,
And the feet of those he fought for,
Echo round his bones for evermore.

III

Lead out the pageant: sad and slow,
As fits an universal woe,
Let the long long procession go,
And let the sorrowing crowd about it grow,
And let the mournful martial music blow;
The last great Englishman is low.

IV

Mourn, for to us he seems the last,
Remembering all his greatness in the Past.
No more in soldier fashion will he greet
With lifted hand the gazer in the street.
O friends, our chief state-oracle is mute:

Mourn for the man of long-enduring blood,
The statesman-warrior, moderate, resolute,
Whole in himself, a common good.
Mourn for the man of amplest influence,
Yet clearest of ambitious crime,
Our greatest yet with least pretence,
Great in council and great in war,
Foremost captain of his time,
Rich in saving common-sense,
And, as the greatest only are,
In his simplicity sublime.
O good gray head which all men knew,
O voice from which their omens all men drew,
O iron nerve to true occasion true,
O fall'n at length that tower of strength
Which stood four-square to all the winds that blew !
Such was he whom we deplore.
The long self-sacrifice of life is o'er.
The great World-victor's victor will be seen no more.

V

All is over and done :
Render thanks to the Giver,
England, for thy son.
Let the bell be toll'd.
Render thanks to the Giver,
And render him to the mould.
Under the cross of gold
That shines over city and river,
There he shall rest for ever
Among the wise and the bold.
Let the bell be toll'd :
And a reverent people behold
The towering car, the sable steeds :
Bright let it be with its blazon'd deeds,
Dark in its funeral fold.
Let the bell be toll'd :
And a deeper knell in the heart be knoll'd ;
And the sound of the sorrowing anthem roll'd
Thro' the dome of the golden cross ;

And the volleying cannon thunder his loss;
He knew their voices of old.
For many a time in many a clime
His captain's-ear has heard them boom
Bellowing victory, bellowing doom:
When he with those deep voices wrought,
Guarding realms and kings from shame;
With those deep voices our dead captain taught
The tyrant, and asserts his claim
In that dread sound to the great name,
Which he has worn so pure of blame,
In praise and in dispraise the same,
A man of well-attemper'd frame.
O civic muse, to such a name,
To such a name for ages long,
To such a name,
Preserve a broad approach of fame,
And ever-echoing avenues of song.

VI

Who is he that cometh, like an honour'd guest,
With banner and with music, with soldier and
    with priest,
With a nation weeping, and breaking on my rest?
Mighty Seaman, this is he
Was great by land as thou by sea.
Thine island loves thee well, thou famous man,
The greatest sailor since our world began.
Now, to the roll of muffled drums
To thee the greatest soldier comes;
For this is he
Was great by land as thou by sea;
His foes were thine; he kept us free;
O give him welcome, this is he
Worthy of our gorgeous rites,
And worthy to be laid by thee;
For this is England's greatest son,
He that gain'd a hundred fights,
Nor ever lost an English gun;
This is he that far away
Against the myriads of Assaye

Clash'd with his fiery few and won;
And underneath another sun,
Warring on a later day,
Round affrighted Lisbon drew
The treble works, the vast designs
Of his labour'd rampart-lines,
Where he greatly stood at bay,
Whence he issued forth anew,
And ever great and greater grew,
Beating from the wasted vines
Back to France her banded swarms,
Back to France with countless blows,
Till o'er the hills her eagles flew
Beyond the Pyrenean pines,
Follow'd up in valley and glen
With blare of bugle, clamour of men,
Roll of cannon and clash of arms,
And England pouring on her foes.
Such a war had such a close.
Again their ravening eagle rose
In anger, wheel'd on Europe-shadowing wings,
And barking for the thrones of kings;
Till one that sought but Duty's iron crown
On that loud sabbath shook the spoiler down;
A day of onsets of despair!
Dash'd on every rocky square
Their surging charges foam'd themselves away;
Last, the Prussian trumpet blew;
Thro' the long-tormented air
Heaven flash'd a sudden jubilant ray,
And down we swept and charged and overthrew.
So great a soldier taught us there,
What long-enduring hearts could do
In that world-earthquake, Waterloo!
Mighty Seaman, tender and true,
And pure as he from taint of craven guile,
O saviour of the silver-coasted isle,
O shaker of the Baltic and the Nile,
If aught of things that here befall
Touch a spirit among things divine,
If love of country move thee there at all,
Be glad, because his bones are laid by thine!

And thro' the centuries let a people's voice
In full acclaim,
A people's voice,
The proof and echo of all human fame,
A people's voice, when they rejoice
At civic revel and pomp and game,
Attest their great commander's claim
With honour, honour, honour, honour to him,
Eternal honour to his name.

VII

A people's voice! we are a people yet.
Tho' all men else their nobler dreams forget,
Confused by brainless mobs and lawless Powers;
Thank Him who isled us here, and roughly set
His Briton in blown seas and storming showers,
We have a voice, with which to pay the debt
Of boundless love and reverence and regret
To those great men who fought, and kept it ours.
And keep it ours, O God, from brute control;
O Statesmen, guard us, guard the eye, the soul
Of Europe, keep our noble England whole,
And save the one true seed of freedom sown
Betwixt a people and their ancient throne,
That sober freedom out of which there springs
Our loyal passion for our temperate kings;
For, saving that, ye help to save mankind
Till public wrong be crumbled into dust,
And drill the raw world for the march of mind,
Till crowds at length be sane and crowns be just.
But wink no more in slothful overtrust.
Remember him who led your hosts;
He bad you guard the sacred coasts.
Your cannons moulder on the seaward wall;
His voice is silent in your council-hall
For ever; and whatever tempests lour
For ever silent; even if they broke
In thunder, silent; yet remember all
He spoke among you, and the Man who spoke;
Who never sold the truth to serve the hour,
Nor palter'd with Eternal God for power;

Who let the turbid streams of rumour flow
Thro' either babbling world of high and low;
Whose life was work, whose language rife
With rugged maxims hewn from life;
Who never spoke against a foe;
Whose eighty winters freeze with one rebuke
All great self-seekers trampling on the right:
Truth-teller was our England's Alfred named;
Truth-lover was our English Duke;
Whatever record leap to light
He never shall be shamed.

VIII

Lo, the leader in these glorious wars
Now to glorious burial slowly borne,
Follow'd by the brave of other lands,
He, on whom from both her open hands
Lavish Honour shower'd all her stars,
And affluent Fortune emptied all her horn.
Yea, let all good things await
Him who cares not to be great,
But as he saves or serves the state.
Not once or twice in our rough island-story,
The path of duty was the way to glory:
He that walks it, only thirsting
For the right, and learns to deaden
Love of self, before his journey closes,
He shall find the stubborn thistle bursting
Into glossy purples, which outredden
All voluptuous garden-roses.
Not once or twice in our fair island-story,
The path of duty was the way to glory:
He, that ever following her commands,
On with toil of heart and knees and hands,
Thro' the long gorge to the far light has won
His path upward, and prevail'd,
Shall find the toppling crags of Duty scaled
Are close upon the shining table-lands
To which our God Himself is moon and sun.
Such was he: his work is done.
But while the races of mankind endure,

Let his great example stand
Colossal, seen of every land,
And keep the soldier firm, the statesman pure:
Till in all lands and thro' all human story
The path of duty be the way to glory:
And let the land whose hearths he saved from shame
For many and many an age proclaim
At civic revel and pomp and game,
And when the long-illumined cities flame,
Their ever-loyal iron leader's fame,
With honour, honour, honour, honour to him,
Eternal honour to his name.

IX

Peace, his triumph will be sung
By some yet unmoulded tongue
Far on in summers that we shall not see:
Peace, it is a day of pain
For one about whose patriarchal knee
Late the little children clung:
O peace, it is a day of pain
For one, upon whose hand and heart and brain
Once the weight and fate of Europe hung.
Ours the pain, be his the gain!
More than is of man's degree
Must be with us, watching here
At this, our great solemnity.
Whom we see not we revere;
We revere, and we refrain
From talk of battles loud and vain,
And brawling memories all too free
For such a wise humility
As befits a solemn fane:
We revere, and while we hear
The tides of Music's golden sea
Setting toward eternity,
Uplifted high in heart and hope are we,
Until we doubt not that for one so true
There must be other nobler work to do
Than when he fought at Waterloo,
And Victor he must ever be.

For tho' the Giant Ages heave the hill
And break the shore, and evermore
Make and break, and work their will;
Tho' world on world in myriad myriads roll
Round us, each with different powers,
And other forms of life than ours,
What know we greater than the soul?
On God and Godlike men we build our trust.
Hush, the Dead March wails in the people's ears:
The dark crowd moves, and there are sobs and
    tears:
The black earth yawns: the mortal disappears;
Ashes to ashes, dust to dust;
He is gone who seem'd so great.—
Gone; but nothing can bereave him
Of the force he made his own
Being here, and we believe him
Something far advanced in State,
And that he wears a truer crown
Than any wreath that man can weave him.
Speak no more of his renown,
Lay your earthly fancies down,
And in the vast cathedral leave him.
God accept him, Christ receive him.

1852

LXVII

THE CHARGE OF THE LIGHT BRIGADE

I

Half a league, half a league,
  Half a league onward,
All in the valley of Death
  Rode the six hundred.
'Forward, the Light Brigade!
Charge for the guns!' he said:
Into the valley of Death
  Rode the six hundred.

II

'Forward, the Light Brigade!'
Was there a man dismay'd?
Not tho' the soldier knew
   Some one had blunder'd:
Their's not to make reply,
Their's not to reason why,
Their's but to do and die:
Into the valley of Death
   Rode the six hundred.

III

Cannon to right of them,
Cannon to left of them,
Cannon in front of them
   Volley'd and thunder'd;
Storm'd at with shot and shell,
Boldly they rode and well,
Into the jaws of Death,
Into the mouth of Hell
   Rode the six hundred.

IV

Flash'd all their sabres bare,
Flash'd as they turn'd in air
Sabring the gunners there,
Charging an army, while
   All the world wonder'd:
Plunged in the battery-smoke
Right thro' the line they broke;
Cossack and Russian
Reel'd from the sabre-stroke
   Shatter'd and sunder'd.
Then they rode back, but not
   Not the six hundred.

V

Cannon to right of them,
Cannon to left of them,
Cannon behind them
   Volley'd and thunder'd;

Storm'd at with shot and shell,
While horse and hero fell,
They that had fought so well
Came thro' the jaws of Death,
Back from the mouth of Hell,
All that was left of them,
  Left of six hundred.

VI

When can their glory fade?
O the wild charge they made!
  All the world wonder'd.
Honour the charge they made!
Honour the Light Brigade,
  Noble six hundred!

LXVIII

THE DEFENCE OF LUCKNOW

I

BANNER of England, not for a season, O banner of Britain, hast thou
Floated in conquering battle or flapt to the battle-cry!
Never with mightier glory than when we had rear'd thee on high
Flying at top of the roofs in the ghastly siege of Lucknow—
Shot thro' the staff or the halyard, but ever we raised thee anew,
And ever upon the topmost roof our banner of England blew.

II

Frail were the works that defended the hold that we held with our lives—
Women and children among us, God help them, our children and wives!
Hold it we might—and for fifteen days or for twenty at most.

P

'Never surrender, I charge you, but every man die at his post!'
Voice of the dead whom we loved, our Lawrence the best of the brave
Cold were his brows when we kiss'd him—we laid him that night in his grave.
'Every man die at his post!' and there hail'd on our houses and halls
Death from their rifle-bullets, and death from their cannon-balls,
Death in our innermost chamber, and death at our slight barricade,
Death while we stood with the musket, and death while we stoopt to the spade,
Death to the dying, and wounds to the wounded, for often there fell,
Striking the hospital wall, crashing thro' it, their shot and their shell,
Death—for their spies were among us, their marksmen were told of our best,
So that the brute bullet broke thro' the brain that could think for the rest;
Bullets would sing by our foreheads, and bullets would rain at our feet—
Fire from ten thousand at once of the rebels that girdled us round—
Death at the glimpse of a finger from over the breadth of a street,
Death from the heights of the mosque and the palace, and death in the ground!
Mine? yes, a mine! Countermine! down, down! and creep thro' the hole!
Keep the revolver in hand! you can hear him—the murderous mole!
Quiet, ah! quiet—wait till the point of the pickaxe be thro'!
Click with the pick, coming nearer and nearer again than before—
Now let it speak, and you fire, and the dark pioneer is no more;
And ever upon the topmost roof our banner of England blew!

III

Ay, but the foe sprung his mine many times, and it
    chanced on a day
Soon as the blast of that underground thunderclap
    echo'd away,
Dark thro' the smoke and the sulphur like so many
    fiends in their hell—
Cannon-shot, musket-shot, volley on volley, and yell
    upon yell—
Fiercely on all the defences our myriad enemy fell.
What have they done? where is it? Out yonder.
    Guard the Redan!
Storm at the Water-gate! storm at the Bailey-gate!
    storm, and it ran
Surging and swaying all round us, as ocean on every
    side
Plunges and heaves at a bank that is daily drown'd
    by the tide—
So many thousands that if they be bold enough, who
    shall escape?
Kill or be kill'd, live or die, they shall know we are
    soldiers and men!
Ready! take aim at their leaders—their masses are
    gapp'd with our grape—
Backward they reel like the wave, like the wave
    flinging forward again,
Flying and foil'd at the last by the handful they could
    not subdue;
And ever upon the topmost roof our banner of
    England blew.

IV

Handful of men as we were, we were English in
    heart and in limb,
Strong with the strength of the race to command, to
    obey, to endure,
Each of us fought as if hope for the garrison hung but
    on him;
Still—could we watch at all points? we were every
    day fewer and fewer.

There was a whisper among us, but only a whisper
    that past:
'Children and wives—if the tigers leap into the fold
    unawares—
Every man die at his post—and the foe may outlive
    us at last—
Better to fall by the hands that they love, than to fall
    into theirs!'
Roar upon roar in a moment two mines by the enemy
    sprung
Clove into perilous chasms our walls and our poor
    palisades.
Rifleman, true is your heart, but be sure that your
    hand be as true!
Sharp is the fire of assault, better aimed are your
    flank fusillades—
Twice do we hurl them to earth from the ladders to
    which they had clung,
Twice from the ditch where they shelter we drive
    them with hand-grenades;
And ever upon the topmost roof our banner of
    England blew.

V

Then on another wild morning another wild earth-
    quake out-tore
Clean from our lines of defence ten or twelve good
    paces or more.
Rifleman, high on the roof, hidden there from the
    light of the sun—
One has leapt up on the breach, crying out: 'Follow
    me, follow me!'—
Mark him—he falls! then another, and *him* too, and
    down goes he.
Had they been bold enough then, who can tell but
    the traitors had won?
Boardings and rafters and doors—an embrasure!
    make way for the gun!
Now double-charge it with grape! It is charged and
    we fire, and they run.
Praise to our Indian brothers, and let the dark face
    have his due!

Thanks to the kindly dark faces who fought with us,
    faithful and few,
Fought with the bravest among us, and drove them,
    and smote them, and slew,
That ever upon the topmost roof our banner in India
    blew.

VI

Men will forget what we suffer and not what we do.
    We can fight !
But to be soldier all day and be sentinel all thro' the
    night—
Ever the mine and assault, our sallies, their lying
    alarms,
Bugles and drums in the darkness, and shoutings and
    soundings to arms,
Ever the labour of fifty that had to be done by five,
Ever the marvel among us that one should be left
    alive,
Ever the day with its traitorous death from the loop-
    holes around,
Ever the night with its coffinless corpse to be laid in
    the ground,
Heat like the mouth of a hell, or a deluge of cataract
    skies,
Stench of old offal decaying, and infinite torment of
    flies,
Thoughts of the breezes of May blowing over an
    English field,
Cholera, scurvy, and fever, the wound that *would* not
    be heal'd,
Lopping away of the limb by the pitiful-pitiless knife,—
Torture and trouble in vain,—for it never could save
    us a life.
Valour of delicate women who tended the hospital bed,
Horror of women in travail among the dying and
    dead,
Grief for our perishing children, and never a moment
    for grief,
Toil and ineffable weariness, faltering hopes of relief,
Havelock baffled, or beaten, or butcher'd for all that
    we knew—

Then day and night, day and night, coming down on
  the still-shatter'd walls
Millions of musket-bullets, and thousands of cannon-
  balls—
But ever upon the topmost roof our banner of
  England blew.

VII

Hark cannonade, fusillade! is it true what was told
  by the scout,
Outram and Havelock breaking their way through the
  fell mutineers?
Surely the pibroch of Europe is ringing again in our ears!
All on a sudden the garrison utter a jubilant shout,
Havelock's glorious Highlanders answer with con-
  quering cheers,
Sick from the hospital echo them, women and children
  come out,
Blessing the wholesome white faces of Havelock's
  good fusileers,
Kissing the war-harden'd hand of the Highlander wet
  with their tears!
Dance to the pibroch!—saved! we are saved!—is it
  you? is it you?
Saved by the valour of Havelock, saved by the bless-
  ing of Heaven!
'Hold it for fifteen days!' we have held it for eighty-
  seven!
And ever aloft on the palace roof the old banner of
  England blew.

LXIX

BREAK, break, break,
  On thy cold gray stones, O Sea!
And I would that my tongue could utter
  The thoughts that arise in me.

O well for the fisherman's boy,
  That he shouts with his sister at play!
O well for the sailor lad,
  That he sings in his boat on the bay!

>   And the stately ships go on
>   To their haven under the hill;
>   But O for the touch of a vanish'd hand,
>   And the sound of a voice that is still!
>
>   Break, break, break,
>   At the foot of thy crags, O Sea!
>   But the tender grace of a day that is dead
>   Will never come back to me.

LXX

IN THE VALLEY OF CAUTERETZ

ALL along the valley, stream that flashest white,
Deepening thy voice with the deepening of the night,
All along the valley, where thy waters flow,
I walk'd with one I loved two and thirty years ago.
All along the valley, while I walk'd to-day,
The two and thirty years were a mist that rolls away;
For all along the valley, down thy rocky bed,
Thy living voice to me was as the voice of the dead,
And all along the valley, by rock and cave and tree,
The voice of the dead was a living voice to me.

In Memoriam

LXXI

>   THIS truth came borne with bier and pall,
>   I felt it, when I sorrow'd most,
>   'Tis better to have loved and lost,
>   Than never to have loved at all——
>
>   O true in word, and tried in deed,
>   Demanding, so to bring relief
>   To this which is our common grief,
>   What kind of life is that I lead;
>
>   And whether trust in things above
>   Be dimm'd of sorrow, or sustain'd:
>   And whether love for him have drain'd
>   My capabilities of love;

Your words have virtue such as draws
    A faithful answer from the breast,
    Thro' light reproaches, half exprest,
And loyal unto kindly laws.

My blood an even tenor kept,
    Till on mine ear this message falls,
    That in Vienna's fatal walls
God's finger touch'd him, and he slept.

The great Intelligences fair
    That range above our mortal state,
    In circle round the blessed gate,
Received and gave him welcome there;

And led him thro' the blissful climes,
    And show'd him in the fountain fresh
    All knowledge that the sons of flesh
Shall gather in the cycled times.

But I remain'd, whose hopes were dim,
    Whose life, whose thoughts were little worth,
    To wander on a darken'd earth,
Where all things round me breathed of him.

O friendship, equal-poised control,
    O heart, with kindliest motion warm,
    O sacred essence, other form,
O solemn ghost, O crowned soul!

Yet none could better know than I,
    How much of act at human hands
    The sense of human will demands
By which we dare to live or die.

Whatever way my days decline,
    I felt and feel, tho' left alone,
    His being working in mine own,
The footsteps of his life in mine;

A life that all the Muses deck'd
    With gifts of grace, that might express
    All-comprehensive tenderness,
All-subtilising intellect:

And so my passion hath not swerved
    To works of weakness, but I find
    An image comforting the mind,
And in my grief a strength reserved.

Likewise the imaginative woe,
    That loved to handle spiritual strife,
    Diffused the shock thro' all my life,
But in the present broke the blow.

My pulses therefore beat again
    For other friends that once I met;
    Nor can it suit me to forget
The mighty hopes that make us men.

I woo your love: I count it crime
    To mourn for any overmuch;
    I, the divided half of such
A friendship as had master'd Time;

Which masters Time indeed, and is
    Eternal, separate from fears:
    The all-assuming months and years
Can take no part away from this:

But Summer on the steaming floods,
    And Spring that swells the narrow brooks,
    And Autumn, with a noise of rooks,
That gather in the waning woods,

And every pulse of wind and wave
    Recalls, in change of light or gloom,
    My old affection of the tomb,
And my prime passion in the grave

My old affection of the tomb,
    A part of stillness, yearns to speak:
    'Arise, and get thee forth and seek
A friendship for the years to come.

'I watch thee from the quiet shore;
    Thy spirit up to mine can reach;
    But in dear words of human speech
We two communicate no more.'

And I, ' Can clouds of nature stain
    The starry clearness of the free?
    How is it? Canst thou feel for me
Some painless sympathy with pain?'

And lightly does the whisper fall;
    ' 'Tis hard for thee to fathom this;
    I triumph in conclusive bliss,
And that serene result of all.'

So hold I commerce with the dead;
    Or so methinks the dead would say;
    Or so shall grief with symbols play
And pining life be fancy-fed.

Now looking to some settled end,
    That these things pass, and I shall prove
    A meeting somewhere, love with love,
I crave your pardon, O my friend;

If not so fresh, with love as true,
    I, clasping brother-hands, aver
    I could not, if I would, transfer
The whole I felt for him to you.

For which be they that hold apart
    The promise of the golden hours?
    First love, first friendship, equal powers,
That marry with the virgin heart.

Still mine, that cannot but deplore,
    That beats within a lonely place,
    That yet remembers his embrace,
But at his footstep leaps no more,

My heart, tho' widow'd, may not rest
    Quite in the love of what is gone,
    But seeks to beat in time with one
That warms another living breast.

Ah, take the imperfect gift I bring,
    Knowing the primrose yet is dear,
    The primrose of the later year,
As not unlike to that of Spring.

LXXII

I HEAR the noise about thy keel;
    I hear the bell struck in the night:
    I see the cabin-window bright;
I see the sailor at the wheel.

Thou bring'st the sailor to his wife,
    And travell'd men from foreign lands;
    And letters unto trembling hands;
And, thy dark freight, a vanish'd life.

So bring him: we have idle dreams:
    This look of quiet flatters thus
    Our home-bred fancies: O to us,
The fools of habit, sweeter seems

To rest beneath the clover sod,
    That takes the sunshine and the rains,
    Or where the kneeling hamlet drains
The chalice of the grapes of God;

Than if with thee the roaring wells
    Should gulf him fathom-deep in brine;
    And hands so often clasp'd in mine,
Should toss with tangle and with shells.

LXXIII

CALM is the morn without a sound,
    Calm as to suit a calmer grief,
    And only thro' the faded leaf
The chestnut pattering to the ground:

Calm and deep peace on this high wold,
    And on these dews that drench the furze,
    And all the silvery gossamers
That twinkle into green and gold:

Calm and still light on yon great plain
    That sweeps with all its autumn bowers,
    And crowded farms and lessening towers,
To mingle with the bounding main:

Calm and deep peace in this wide air,
    These leaves that redden to the fall;
    And in my heart, if calm at all,
If any calm, a calm despair:

Calm on the seas, and silver sleep,
    And waves that sway themselves in rest,
    And dead calm in that noble breast
Which heaves but with the heaving deep.

LXXIV

Tears of the widower, when he sees
    A late-lost form that sleep reveals,
    And moves his doubtful arms, and feels
Her place is empty, fall like these;

Which weep a loss for ever new,
    A void where heart on heart reposed;
    And, where warm hands have prest and closed,
Silence, till I be silent too.

Which weep the comrade of my choice,
    An awful thought, a life removed,
    The human-hearted man I loved,
A Spirit, not a breathing voice.

Come Time, and teach me, many years,
    I do not suffer in a dream;
    For now so strange do these things seem,
Mine eyes have leisure for their tears;

My fancies time to rise on wing,
    And glance about the approaching sails,
    As tho' they brought but merchants' bales,
And not the burthen that they bring.

LXXV

If one should bring me this report,
    That thou hadst touch'd the land to-day,
    And I went down unto the quay,
And found thee lying in the port;

And standing, muffled round with woe,
    Should see thy passengers in rank
    Come stepping lightly down the plank,
And beckoning unto those they know;

And if along with these should come
    The man I held as half-divine;
    Should strike a sudden hand in mine,
And ask a thousand things of home;

And I should tell him all my pain,
    And how my life had droop'd of late,
    And he should sorrow o'er my state
And marvel what possess'd my brain;

And I perceived no touch of change,
    No hint of death in all his frame,
    But found him all in all the same,
I should not feel it to be strange.

LXXVI

'Tis well; 'tis something; we may stand
    Where he in English earth is laid,
    And from his ashes may be made
The violet of his native land.

'Tis little; but it looks in truth
    As if the quiet bones were blest
    Among familiar names to rest
And in the places of his youth.

Come then, pure hands, and bear the head
    That sleeps or wears the mask of sleep,
    And come, whatever loves to weep,
And hear the ritual of the dead.

Ah yet, ev'n yet, if this might be,
    I, falling on his faithful heart,
    Would breathing thro' his lips impart
The life that almost dies in me;

That dies not, but endures with pain,
    And slowly forms the firmer mind,
    Treasuring the look it cannot find,
The words that are not heard again.

LXXVII

THE Danube to the Severn gave
    The darken'd heart that beat no more;
    They laid him by the pleasant shore,
And in the hearing of the wave.

There twice a day the Severn fills;
    The salt sea-water passes by,
    And hushes half the babbling Wye,
And makes a silence in the hills.

The Wye is hush'd nor moved along,
    And hush'd my deepest grief of all,
    When fill'd with tears that cannot fall,
I brim with sorrow drowning song.

The tide flows down, the wave again
    Is vocal in its wooded walls;
    My deeper anguish also falls,
And I can speak a little then.

LXXVIII

WITH weary steps I loiter on,
    Tho' always under alter'd skies
    The purple from the distance dies,
My prospect and horizon gone.

No joy the blowing season gives,
    The herald melodies of spring,
    But in the songs I love to sing
A doubtful gleam of solace lives.

If any care for what is here
    Survive in spirits render'd free,
    Then are these songs I sing of thee
Not all ungrateful to thine ear.

LXXIX

PEACE; come away: the song of woe
    Is after all an earthly song:
    Peace; come away: we do him wrong
To sing so wildly: let us go.

Come; let us go: your cheeks are pale;
    But half my life I leave behind:
    Methinks my friend is richly shrined;
But I shall pass; my work will fail.

Yet in these ears, till hearing dies,
    One set slow bell will seem to toll
    The passing of the sweetest soul
That ever look'd with human eyes.

I hear it now, and o'er and o'er,
    Eternal greetings to the dead;
    And 'Ave, Ave, Ave,' said,
'Adieu, adieu' for evermore.

LXXX

IN those sad words I took farewell:
    Like echoes in sepulchral halls,
    As drop by drop the water falls
In vaults and catacombs, they fell;

And, falling, idly broke the peace
    Of hearts that beat from day to day,
    Half-conscious of their dying clay,
And those cold crypts where they shall cease.

The high Muse answer'd: 'Wherefore grieve
  Thy brethren with a fruitless tear?
  Abide a little longer here,
And thou shalt take a nobler leave.'

LXXXI

As sometimes in a dead man's face,
  To those that watch it more and more,
  A likeness, hardly seen before,
Comes out—to some one of his race:

So, dearest, now thy brows are cold,
  I see thee what thou art, and know
  Thy likeness to the wise below,
Thy kindred with the great of old.

But there is more than I can see,
  And what I see I leave unsaid,
  Nor speak it knowing Death has made
His darkness beautiful with thee.

LXXXII

He tasted love with half his mind,
  Nor ever drank the inviolate spring
  Where nighest heaven, who first could fling
This bitter seed among mankind;

That could the dead, whose dying eyes
  Were closed with wail, resume their life,
  They would but find in child and wife
An iron welcome when they rise:

'Twas well, indeed, when warm with wine,
  To pledge them with a kindly tear,
  To talk them o'er, to wish them here,
To count their memories half divine;

But if they came who past away,
  Behold their brides in other hands;
  The hard heir strides about their lands,
And will not yield them for a day.

Yea, tho' their sons were none of these,
    Not less the yet-loved sire would make
    Confusion worse than death, and shake
The pillars of domestic peace.

Ah dear, but come thou back to me:
    Whatever change the years have wrought,
    I find not yet one lonely thought
That cries against my wish for thee.

LXXXIII

When rosy plumelets tuft the larch,
    And rarely pipes the mounted thrush;
    Or underneath the barren bush
Flits by the sea-blue bird of March;

Come, wear the form by which I know
    Thy spirit in time among thy peers;
    The hope of unaccomplish'd years
Be large and lucid round thy brow.

When summer's hourly-mellowing change
    May breathe, with many roses sweet,
    Upon the thousand waves of wheat,
That ripple round the lonely grange;

Come: not in watches of the night,
    But where the sunbeam broodeth warm,
    Come, beauteous in thine after form,
And like a finer light in light.

LXXXIV

Now fades the last long streak of snow,
    Now burgeons every maze of quick
    About the flowering squares, and thick
By ashen roots the violets blow.

Now rings the woodland loud and long,
    The distance takes a lovelier hue,
    And drown'd in yonder living blue
The lark becomes a sightless song.

Now dance the lights on lawn and lea,
    The flocks are whiter down the vale,
    And milkier every milky sail
On winding stream or distant sea;

Where now the seamew pipes, or dives
    In yonder greening gleam, and fly
    The happy birds, that change their sky
To build and brood; that live their lives

From land to land; and in my breast
    Spring wakens too; and my regret
    Becomes an April violet,
And buds and blossoms like the rest.

LXXXV

Is it, then, regret for buried time
    That keenlier in sweet April wakes,
    And meets the year, and gives and takes
The colours of the crescent prime?

Not all: the songs, the stirring air,
    The life re-orient out of dust,
    Cry thro' the sense to hearten trust
In that which made the world so fair.

Not all regret: the face will shine
    Upon me, while I muse alone;
    And that dear voice, I once have known,
Still speak to me of me and mine:

Yet less of sorrow lives in me
    For days of happy commune dead;
    Less yearning for the friendship fled,
Than some strong bond which is to be.

LXXXVI

DOORS, where my heart was used to beat
    So quickly, not as one that weeps
    I come once more; the city sleeps;
I smell the meadow in the street;

I hear a chirp of birds; I see
    Betwixt the black fronts long-withdrawn
    A light-blue lane of early dawn,
And think of early days and thee,

And bless thee, for thy lips are bland,
    And bright the friendship of thine eye;
    And in my thoughts with scarce a sigh
I take the pressure of thine hand.

LXXXVII

THERE rolls the deep where grew the tree.
    O earth, what changes hast thou seen!
    There where the long street roars, hath been
The stillness of the central sea.

The hills are shadows, and they flow
    From form to form, and nothing stands;
    They melt like mist, the solid lands,
Like clouds they shape themselves and go.

But in my spirit will I dwell,
    And dream my dream, and hold it true;
    For tho' my lips may breathe adieu,
I cannot think the thing farewell.

LXXXVIII

OLD Yew, which graspest at the stones
    That name the under-lying dead,
    Thy fibres net the dreamless head,
Thy roots are wrapt about the bones.

The seasons bring the flower again,
    And bring the firstling to the flock;
    And in the dusk of thee, the clock
Beats out the little lives of men.

O not for thee the glow, the bloom,
    Who changest not in any gale,
    Nor branding summer suns avail
To touch thy thousand years of gloom:

And gazing on thee, sullen tree,
  Sick for thy stubborn hardihood,
  I seem to fail from out my blood
And grow incorporate into thee.

LXXXIX

One writes, that 'Other friends remain,'
  That 'Loss is common to the race'—
  And common is the commonplace,
And vacant chaff well meant for grain.

That loss is common would not make
  My own less bitter, rather more:
  Too common! Never morning wore
To evening, but some heart did break.

O father, wheresoe'er thou be,
  Who pledgest now thy gallant son;
  A shot, ere half thy draught be done,
Hath still'd the life that beat from thee.

O mother, praying God will save
  Thy sailor,—while thy head is bow'd,
  His heavy-shotted hammock-shroud
Drops in his vast and wandering grave.

Ye know no more than I who wrought
  At that last hour to please him well;
  Who mused on all I had to tell,
And something written, something thought;

Expecting still his advent home;
  And ever met him on his way
  With wishes, thinking, 'here to-day,'
Or 'here to-morrow will he come.'

O somewhere, meek, unconscious dove,
  That sittest ranging golden hair;
  And glad to find thyself so fair,
Poor child, that waitest for thy love!

For now her father's chimney glows
    In expectation of a guest;
      And thinking 'this will please him best,'
She takes a riband or a rose;

For he will see them on to-night;
    And with the thought her colour burns;
      And, having left the glass, she turns
Once more to set a ringlet right;

And, even when she turn'd, the curse
    Had fallen, and her future Lord
      Was drown'd in passing thro' the ford,
Or kill'd in falling from his horse.

O what to her shall be the end?
    And what to me remains of good?
      To her, perpetual maidenhood,
And unto me no second friend.

XC

THE lesser griefs that may be said,
    That breathe a thousand tender vows,
      Are but as servants in a house
Where lies the master newly dead;

Who speak their feeling as it is,
    And weep the fulness from the mind:
      'It will be hard,' they say, 'to find
Another service such as this.'

My lighter moods are like to these,
    That out of words a comfort win;
      But there are other griefs within,
And tears that at their fountain freeze;

For by the hearth the children sit
    Cold in that atmosphere of Death,
      And scarce endure to draw the breath,
Or like to noiseless phantoms flit:

But open converse is there none,
    So much the vital spirits sink
    To see the vacant chair, and think,
'How good! how kind! and he is gone.'

XCI

I ENVY not in any moods
    The captive void of noble rage,
    The linnet born within the cage,
That never knew the summer woods:

I envy not the beast that takes
    His license in the field of time,
    Unfetter'd by the sense of crime,
To whom a conscience never wakes;

Nor, what may count itself as blest,
    The heart that never plighted troth
    But stagnates in the weeds of sloth;
Nor any want-begotten rest.

I hold it true, whate'er befall;
    I feel it, when I sorrow most;
    'Tis better to have loved and lost
Than never to have loved at all.

XCII

THE time draws near the birth of Christ:
    The moon is hid; the night is still;
    The Christmas bells from hill to hill
Answer each other in the mist.

Four voices of four hamlets round,
    From far and near, on mead and moor,
    Swell out and fail, as if a door
Were shut between me and the sound:

Each voice four changes on the wind,
    That now dilate, and now decrease,
    Peace and goodwill, goodwill and peace,
Peace and goodwill, to all mankind.

This year I slept and woke with pain,
    I almost wish'd no more to wake,
      And that my hold on life would break
Before I heard those bells again :

But they my troubled spirit rule,
    For they controll'd me when a boy ;
      They bring me sorrow touch'd with joy,
The merry merry bells of Yule.

XCIII

WHEN Lazarus left his charnel-cave,
    And home to Mary's house return'd,
      Was this demanded—if he yearn'd
To hear her weeping by his grave?

'Where wert thou, brother, those four days?'
    There lives no record of reply,
      Which telling what it is to die
Had surely added praise to praise.

From every house the neighbours met,
    The streets were fill'd with joyful sound,
      A solemn gladness even crown'd
The purple brows of Olivet.

Behold a man raised up by Christ !
    The rest remaineth unreveal'd ;
      He told it not; or something seal'd
The lips of that Evangelist.

XCIV

HER eyes are homes of silent prayer,
    Nor other thought her mind admits
      But, he was dead, and there he sits,
And he that brought him back is there.

Then one deep love doth supersede
    All other, when her ardent gaze
      Roves from the living brother's face,
And rests upon the Life indeed.

All subtle thought, all curious fears,
  Borne down by gladness so complete,
  She bows, she bathes the Saviour's feet
With costly spikenard and with tears.

Thrice blest whose lives are faithful prayers,
  Whose loves in higher love endure;
  What souls possess themselves so pure,
Or is there blessedness like theirs?

XCV

O THOU that after toil and storm
  Mayst seem to have reach'd a purer air,
  Whose faith has centre everywhere,
Nor cares to fix itself to form,

Leave thou thy sister when she prays,
  Her early Heaven, her happy views;
  Nor thou with shadow'd hint confuse
A life that leads melodious days.

Her faith thro' form is pure as thine,
  Her hands are quicker unto good:
  Oh, sacred be the flesh and blood
To which she links a truth divine!

See thou, that countest reason ripe
  In holding by the law within,
  Thou fail not in a world of sin,
And ev'n for want of such a type.

XCVI

THO' truths in manhood darkly join,
  Deep-seated in our mystic frame,
  We yield all blessing to the name
Of Him that made them current coin;

For Wisdom dealt with mortal powers,
  Where truth in closest words shall fail,
  When truth embodied in a tale
Shall enter in at lowly doors.

And so the Word had breath, and wrought
    With human hands the creed of creeds
    In loveliness of perfect deeds,
More strong than all poetic thought

Which he may read that binds the sheaf,
    Or builds the house, or digs the grave,
    And those wild eyes that watch the wave
In roarings round the coral reef.

XCVII

COULD we forget the widow'd hour
    And look on Spirits breathed away,
    As on a maiden in the day
When first she wears her orange-flower !

When crown'd with blessing she doth rise
    To take her latest leave of home,
    And hopes and light regrets that come
Make April of her tender eyes ;

And doubtful joys the father move,
    And tears are on the mother's face,
    As parting with a long embrace
She enters other realms of love ;

Her office there to rear, to teach,
    Becoming as is meet and fit
    A link among the days, to knit
The generations each with each ;

And, doubtless, unto thee is given
    A life that bears immortal fruit
    In those great offices that suit
The full-grown energies of heaven.

Ay me, the difference I discern !
    How often shall her old fireside
    Be cheer'd with tidings of the bride,
How often she herself return,

And tell them all they would have told,
    And bring her babe, and make her boast,
    Till even those that miss'd her most
And shall count new things as dear as old:

But thou and I have shaken hands,
    Till growing winters lay me low;
    My paths are in the fields I know,
And thine in undiscover'd lands.

XCVIII

BE near me when my light is low,
    When the blood creeps, and the nerves prick
    And tingle; and the heart is sick,
And all the wheels of Being slow.

Be near me when the sensuous frame
    Is rack'd with pangs that conquer trust;
    And Time, a maniac scattering dust,
And Life, a Fury slinging flame.

Be near me when my faith is dry,
    And men the flies of latter spring,
    That lay their eggs, and sting and sing
And weave their petty cells and die.

Be near me when I fade away,
    To point the term of human strife,
    And on the low dark verge of life
The twilight of eternal day.

XCIX

Do we indeed desire the dead
    Should still be near us at our side?
    Is there no baseness we would hide?
No inner vileness that we dread?

Shall he for whose applause I strove,
    I had such reverence for his blame,
    See with clear eye some hidden shame
And I be lessen'd in his love?

I wrong the grave with fears untrue:
　　Shall love be blamed for want of faith?
　　There must be wisdom with great Death:
The dead shall look me thro' and thro'.

Be near us when we climb or fall:
　　Ye watch, like God, the rolling hours
　　With larger other eyes than ours,
To make allowance for us all.

C

OH yet we trust that somehow good
　　Will be the final goal of ill,
　　To pangs of nature, sins of will,
Defects of doubt, and taints of blood;

That nothing walks with aimless feet;
　　That not one life shall be destroy'd,
　　Or cast as rubbish to the void,
When God hath made the pile complete;

That not a worm is cloven in vain;
　　That not a moth with vain desire
　　Is shrivell'd in a fruitless fire,
Or but subserves another's gain.

Behold, we know not anything;
　　I can but trust that good shall fall
　　At last—far off—at last, to all,
And every winter change to spring.

So runs my dream: but what am I?
　　An infant crying in the night:
　　An infant crying for the light:
And with no language but a cry.

CI

HE past; a soul of nobler tone:
　　My spirit loved and loves him yet,
　　Like some poor girl whose heart is set
On one whose rank exceeds her own.

He mixing with his proper sphere,
    She finds the baseness of her lot,
    Half jealous of she knows not what,
And envying all that meet him there.

The little village looks forlorn;
    She sighs amid her narrow days,
    Moving about the household ways,
In that dark house where she was born.

The foolish neighbours come and go,
    And tease her till the day draws by:
    At night she weeps, 'How vain am I!
How should he love a thing so low?'

CII

Dost thou look back on what hath been,
    As some divinely gifted man,
    Whose life in low estate began
And on a simple village green;

Who breaks his birth's invidious bar,
    And grasps the skirts of happy chance,
    And breasts the blows of circumstance,
And grapples with his evil star;

Who makes by force his merit known
    And lives to clutch the golden keys,
    To mould a mighty state's decrees,
And shape the whisper of the throne;

And moving up from high to higher,
    Becomes on Fortune's crowning slope
    The pillar of a people's hope,
The centre of a world's desire;

Yet feels, as in a pensive dream,
    When all his active powers are still,
    A distant dearness in the hill,
A secret sweetness in the stream,

The limit of his narrower fate,
    While yet beside its vocal springs
    He play'd at counsellors and kings,
With one that was his earliest mate;

Who ploughs with pain his native lea
    And reaps the labour of his hands,
    Or in the furrow musing stands;
'Does my old friend remember me?'

CIII

I DREAM'D there would be Spring no more,
    That Nature's ancient power was lost:
    The streets were black with smoke and frost,
They chatter'd trifles at the door:

I wander'd from the noisy town,
    I found a wood with thorny boughs:
    I took the thorns to bind my brows,
I wore them like a civic crown:

I met with scoffs, I met with scorns
    From youth and babe and hoary hairs:
    They call'd me in the public squares
The fool that wears a crown of thorns:

They call'd me fool, they call'd me child:
    I found an angel of the night;
    The voice was low, the look was bright;
He look'd upon my crown and smiled:

He reach'd the glory of a hand,
    That seem'd to touch it into leaf:
    The voice was not the voice of grief,
The words were hard to understand.

CIV

SWEET after showers, ambrosial air,
    That rollest from the gorgeous gloom
    Of evening over brake and bloom
And meadow, slowly breathing bare

The round of space, and rapt below
    Thro' all the dewy-tassell'd wood,
    And shadowing down the horned flood
In ripples, fan my brows and blow

The fever from my cheek, and sigh
    The full new life that feeds thy breath
    Throughout my frame, till Doubt and Death,
Ill brethren, let the fancy fly

From belt to belt of crimson seas
    On leagues of odour streaming far,
    To where in yonder orient star
A hundred spirits whisper 'Peace.'

CV

How pure at heart and sound in head,
    With what divine affections bold
    Should be the man whose thought would hold
An hour's communion with the dead.

In vain shalt thou, or any, call
    The spirits from their golden day,
    Except, like them, thou too canst say,
My spirit is at peace with all.

They haunt the silence of the breast,
    Imaginations calm and fair,
    The memory like a cloudless air,
The conscience as a sea at rest:

But when the heart is full of din,
    And doubt beside the portal waits,
    They can but listen at the gates,
And hear the household jar within.

CVI

My love has talk'd with rocks and trees;
    He finds on misty mountain-ground
    His own vast shadow glory-crown'd;
He sees himself in all he sees.

Two partners of a married life—
    I look'd on these and thought of thee
    In vastness and in mystery,
And of my spirit as of a wife.

These two—they dwelt with eye on eye,
    Their hearts of old have beat in tune,
    Their meetings made December June,
Their every parting was to die.

Their love has never past away;
    The days she never can forget
    Are earnest that he loves her yet,
Whate'er the faithless people say.

Her life is lone, he sits apart,
    He loves her yet, she will not weep,
    Tho' rapt in matters dark and deep
He seems to slight her simple heart.

He thrids the labyrinth of the mind,
    He reads the secret of the star,
    He seems so near and yet so far,
He looks so cold : she thinks him kind.

She keeps the gift of years before,
    A wither'd violet is her bliss :
    She knows not what his greatness is,
For that, for all, she loves him more.

For him she plays, to him she sings
    Of early faith and plighted vows ;
    She knows but matters of the house,
And he, he knows a thousand things.

Her faith is fixt and cannot move,
    She darkly feels him great and wise,
    She dwells on him with faithful eyes,
'I cannot understand : I love.'

CVII

RISEST thou thus, dim dawn, again,
    So loud with voices of the birds,
    So thick with lowings of the herds,
Day, when I lost the flower of men ;

Who tremblest thro' thy darkling red
    On yon swoll'n brook that bubbles fast
    By meadows breathing of the past,
And woodlands holy to the dead;

Who murmurest in the foliaged eaves
    A song that slights the coming care,
    And Autumn laying here and there
A fiery finger on the leaves;

Who wakenest with thy balmy breath
    To myriads on the genial earth,
    Memories of bridal, or of birth,
And unto myriads more, of death.

O wheresoever those may be,
    Betwixt the slumber of the poles,
    To-day they count as kindred souls;
They know me not, but mourn with me.

CVIII

I CLIMB the hill: from end to end
    Of all the landscape underneath,
    I find no place that does not breathe
Some gracious memory of my friend;

No gray old grange, or lonely fold,
    Or low morass and whispering reed,
    Or simple stile from mead to mead,
Or sheepwalk up the windy wold;

Nor hoary knoll of ash and haw
    That hears the latest linnet trill,
    Nor quarry trench'd along the hill
And haunted by the wrangling daw;

Nor runlet tinkling from the rock;
    Nor pastoral rivulet that swerves
    To left and right thro' meadowy curves,
That feed the mothers of the flock;

But each has pleased a kindred eye,
    And each reflects a kindlier day;
    And, leaving these, to pass away,
I think once more he seems to die.

CIX

UNWATCH'D, the garden bough shall sway,
    The tender blossom flutter down,
    Unloved, that beech will gather brown,
This maple burn itself away;

Unloved, the sun-flower, shining fair,
    Ray round with flames her disc of seed,
    And many a rose-carnation feed
With summer spice the humming air;

Unloved, by many a sandy bar,
    The brook shall babble down the plain,
    At noon or when the lesser wain
Is twisting round the polar star;

Uncared for, gird the windy grove,
    And flood the haunts of hern and crake;
    Or into silver arrows break
The sailing moon in creek and cove;

Till from the garden and the wild
    A fresh association blow,
    And year by year the landscape grow
Familiar to the stranger's child;

As year by year the labourer tills
    His wonted glebe, or lops the glades;
    And year by year our memory fades
From all the circle of the hills.

CX

AGAIN at Christmas did we weave
    The holly round the Christmas hearth;
    The silent snow possess'd the earth,
And calmly fell our Christmas-eve:

The yule-clog sparkled keen with frost,
    No wing of wind the region swept,
    But over all things brooding slept
The quiet sense of something lost.

As in the winters left behind,
    Again our ancient games had place,
    The mimic picture's breathing grace,
And dance and song and hoodman-blind.

Who show'd a token of distress?
    No single tear, no mark of pain:
    O sorrow, then can sorrow wane?
O grief, can grief be changed to less?

O last regret, regret can die!
    No—mixt with all this mystic frame,
    Her deep relations are the same,
But with long use her tears are dry.

CXI

RING out, wild bells, to the wild sky,
    The flying cloud, the frosty light:
    The year is dying in the night;
Ring out, wild bells, and let him die.

Ring out the old, ring in the new,
    Ring, happy bells, across the snow:
    The year is going, let him go;
Ring out the false, ring in the true.

Ring out the grief that saps the mind,
    For those that here we see no more;
    Ring out the feud of rich and poor,
Ring in redress to all mankind.

Ring out a slowly dying cause,
    And ancient forms of party strife;
    Ring in the nobler modes of life,
With sweeter manners, purer laws.

Ring out the want, the care, the sin,
>   The faithless coldness of the times;
>   Ring out, ring out my mournful rhymes,
But ring the fuller minstrel in.

Ring out false pride in place and blood,
>   The civic slander and the spite;
>   Ring in the love of truth and right,
Ring in the common love of good.

Ring out old shapes of foul disease;
>   Ring out the narrowing lust of gold;
>   Ring out the thousand wars of old,
Ring in the thousand years of peace.

Ring in the valiant man and free,
>   The larger heart, the kindlier hand;
>   Ring out the darkness of the land,
Ring in the Christ that is to be.

CXII

O LIVING will that shalt endure
>   When all that seems shall suffer shock,
>   Rise in the spiritual rock,
Flow thro' our deeds and make them pure,

That we may lift from out of dust
>   A voice as unto him that hears,
>   A cry above the conquer'd years
To one that with us works, and trust,

With faith that comes of self-control,
>   The truths that never can be proved
>   Until we close with all we loved,
And all we flow from, soul in soul.

THE END

NOTES

PAGE

3 St. 1 *The Legend of Good Women:* One of Chaucer's unfinished pieces. Of the seventeen heroines named in the Prologue, only nine are dealt with, and among these several bear strong traces of hasty treatment, as if the task, (possibly laid upon him by the Queen Anne), had not been wholly congenial to the Poet. Chaucer, in fact, often displays that Mediaeval bias against Woman, which is in such singular contrast with the contemporaneous attitude of romantic adoration: he lacks the finer chivalrous tone of Dante, Petrarch, or Spenser: "Shakespeare's women," or such as the *Dream* before us presents, are beings hardly known to him. Cleopatra is the single heroine common to the two poems, and it is the Cleopatra of the Play which has been here before Tennyson, not the pale sketch of Chaucer's half-hearted Legend.

— St. 2 *Dan:* ancient for *Dominus*, and used thus of Chaucer by Spenser, who looked up to him as his poetical Master.—P. 4, St. 1 *the tortoise:* name in ancient warfare for a body of shield-covered soldiers, or for a strong shed, moving against the wall of a besieged place to pierce or storm it.

4 St. 8 *an old wood:* image of the Past.—P. 5, St. 1 These lines set forth such a picture as would have suited the style of the great Turner

PAGE
4   in his maturity. St. 7 The first "fair woman" is Helen of Troy: The *one that stood beside*, (P. 6, St. 1), Iphigeneia, sacrificed to Artemis that the Grecian fleet might sail from Aulis to Troy at the beginning of the *iron years* of war. Next (St. 7) follows Cleopatra, described as by Shakespeare (Act 1, Sc. 5)
—Me
That am with Phœbus' amorous pinches black—,
although the *polish'd argent of her breast* (P. 7, St. 7) shows that a lady of Hellenic blood is here intended.—Jeptha's daughter and Fair Rosamond succeed: and as the dream ends, (P. 10, St. 7, 8), Margaret Roper, daughter to Sir Thomas More murdered by Henry VIII, Joan of Arc, and Eleanor Queen of Edward I, pass before us and are gone.

7   St. 4 *Canopus:* a large star in Argo, not visible above the southern part of the Mediterranean.— P. 10, St. 5 *Fulvia:* Antony's first wife, widow to Clodius, an imperious lady;—named here by Cleopatra as a parallel to Eleanor:—St. 6 *The captain of my dreams:* the Morning Star.

11 *The Palace of Art:* A Prologue in blank verse precedes this lyric:
I send you here a sort of allegory,
(For you will understand it) of a soul,
A sinful soul possess'd of many gifts,
A spacious garden full of flowering weeds,
A glorious Devil, large in heart and brain,
That did love Beauty only (Beauty seen
In all varieties of mould and mind)
And Knowledge for its beauty; or if Good,
Good only for its beauty, seeing not
That Beauty, Good, and Knowledge, are three sisters
That doat upon each other, friends to man,
Living together under the same roof,
And never can be sunder'd without tears.
And he that shuts Love out, in turn shall be
Shut out from Love, and on her threshold lie

PAGE
11   Howling in outer darkness. Not for this
        Was common clay ta'en from the common earth
        Moulded by God, and temper'd with the tears
        Of angels to the perfect shape of man.

13   St. 7 *hoary to the wind:* as the olives showed
        the gray underside of their leaves.—P. 14, St. 5
        Uther's son: Arthur.—*Avalon:* used here for
        an unknown fairy region, whither Arthur is
        transported by a queen and many fair ladies:
        (Malory, *Morte d'Arthur*). The origin of this
        name, in its connection with Arthur, when
        closely looked at, presents much curious per-
        plexity. A little changed in sound and accent
        from the Welsh Afállon, and meaning simply
        Apple-trees, — in the legend it stands at once
        for Glastonbury in Somerset, and for that
        mystic island to which Arthur is carried
        by "weeping queens," and whence he is to
        return and deliver his countrymen. Vague and
        scanty as our evidence is, we have strong
        reason to believe that, of these two wholly
        opposed stories of the King's fate, the roman-
        tic Passing of Arthur is much the older: and
        to it, I apprehend, the first employment of
        Avalon, and that in its magical sense, must
        belong.

14   St. 6 *the Ausonian king:* Numa. Ausonia
        was a poetical name for Italy during its mythi-
        cal period. St. 7 *Indian Cama:* the god of
        Love, son to Brahma. He is figured as a
        beautiful youth, accompanied by his wife Rati,
        (the personification of Spring),—by a cuckoo,
        a bee, and refreshing breezes before him. So
        Lucretius:

        It Ver, et Venus, et Veneris praenuntius ante
        Pennatus graditur Zephyrus—

—   St. 8 *Europa's mantle blew: blue* appeared here
        by misprint in several editions.—P. 15, St. 2
        Caucasian mind: used for what are often
        named the Aryan, or the Indo-Germanic races,

PAGE	
14	a term including the Hellenic, Latin, and Celtic. St. 5 *the Ionian father:* Homer.—P. 16, St. 3 *The first of those who know:* Plato and Bacon are both here intended. Nollekens' bust in the library of Trinity College suggested the epithet *large-brow'd*. St. 9 *anadems:* garlands.
18	St. 1 *The abysmal deeps:*—With this may be compared the "abysmal *Ich*" of J. P. Richter, and a phrase from an Essay by Arthur Hallam: "God's election, with whom alone rest the abysmal secrets of personality." St. 6 *fretted foreheads:* worm-eaten: *Fretted* here used in the sense of the German *fressen*. St. 9 *moving Circumstance:* old phrase for the surrounding sphere of the Heavens.

In the first edition (1833) of this Poem was added as a note:—"When I first conceived the plan of the Palace of Art, I intended to have introduced both sculptures and paintings into it; but it is the most difficult of all things to *devise* a statue in verse. Judge whether I have succeeded in the statues of Elijah and Olympias:

> One was the Tishbite whom the raven fed,
>   As when he stood on Carmel-steeps
> With one arm stretch'd out bare, and mock'd and said,
>   "Come, cry aloud—he sleeps!"
>
> Tall, eager, lean, and strong, his cloak wind-borne
>   Behind, his forehead heavenly-bright
> From the clear marble pouring glorious scorn,
>   Lit as with inner light.
>
> One was Olympias: the floating snake
>   Roll'd round her ankles, round her waist
> Knotted, and folded once about her neck,
>   Her perfect lips to taste

PAGE
18   Down by the shoulder moved : she seeming blithe
         Declined her head : on every side
     The dragon's curves melted and mingled with
         The woman's youthful pride

     Of rounded limbs."

Olympias (St. 3) Mother to Alexander the Great : Plutarch tells that she was devoted to the Orphic rites, and "was wont in the dances proper to these ceremonies to have great tame serpents about her."

In the same edition, the following stanzas,—inserted before St. 7, P. 17, were meant to be "expressive of the joy wherewith the soul contemplated the results of astronomical experiment. In the centre of the four quadrangles rose an immense tower :—

Hither, when all the deep unsounded skies
    Shudder'd with silent stars, she clomb,
And as with optic glasses her keen eyes
    Pierced through the mystic dome,

Regions of lucid matter taking forms,
    Brushes of fire, hazy gleams,
Clusters and beds of worlds, and bee-like swarms
    Of suns, and starry streams.

She saw the snowy poles and moons of Mars,
    That marvellous field of drifted light
In mid Orion, and the married stars—"

*   *   *   *   *

St. 2 refers to the nebular systems as the most powerful telescopes reveal them. —The *moons of Mars* (St. 3) :—a later correction by the author : under whose permission the preceding stanzas are here reprinted.

20   III St. 2 *dreary gleams:* of flying light.—P. 24, St. 4 *the poet sings:* Dante, *Inferno,* c. v :

         Nessun maggior dolore
     Che ricordarsi del tempo felice
     Nella miseria.

PAGE

26   St. 5 *dreary dawn:* an effect which must have been often noticed when approaching London on the top of the mail-coach in old days.—P. 30, St. 4 *a cycle of Cathay:* any number of years of what is popularly described as Chinese immobility.

32   IV St. 3 *cuckoo-flowers:* One of the Bitter-Cresses; *Cardamine pratensis* of Linnaeus.—P. 33, St. 4 *Charles's Wain:* the Great Bear.

38   *In the Children's Hospital:*—It should be remembered that this is a little drama, in which the Hospital Nurse, not the Poet, is supposed to be speaking throughout. The two children, whose story was published in a Parish Magazine, are the only characters here described from actual life.

On the respective merits of the pieces printed in this book it would, in general, be out of place to offer comment. But I cannot refrain from adding that this is the most absolutely pathetic poem known to me;—as the two which follow may, perhaps, be reckoned the most Shakespearean of the Author's lyrics.

—   St. 1 *oorali:* also *curari*, or *woorali*—a drug extracted from *Strychnos toxifera:*—It acts by paralysing the nerves of motion, whilst the sensitiveness is left unimpaired.

48   *Rizpah.* Highway robbery during the eighteenth century was a crime so rife in England, and one so seriously hostile to private and public interests, that the law, for a time, became perhaps over-severe in the attempt to repress it. The corpses of those convicted were hung in chains near the scene of their robbery:—the last relic of a mode of punishment traceable to very early times. Turner,—always alive to any human interest connected with landscape,—has not omitted to place the gallows on the summit of Hind Head, in his view of that hill in the *Liber Studiorum*, whilst the mail is passing safely along the highway.

PAGE	
54	*The Vision of Sin.* In this lyric,—which belongs to the maturity of the poet's first style, as *Rizpah* and the *Hospital* are masterpieces of his latest,—we first see the winged Soul of a youth who, allured by pleasure, yields himself up to a Pagan-Renaissance Epicurean life, blind to God and the After-world, and the daily displayed signs of their existence. The heavy cloud of satiety and exhaustion, by a law which is at once natural and divine, hence gradually enshrouds him.—Then the vision changes: a vividly realistic picture replaces the symbolical imagery of the Prologue: the selfish sensuality of Youth is shown transmuted into the cynical selfishness of Age, in the person of the traveller who recites his bitter creed of negations,—with a prosaic plainness of speech strangely set to the music of perfect lyrical expression. This Feast of Death, in which other lost souls join, ends with a return to the landscape mystically symbolizing the World after Death, and figuring the final fate of Sin.

The lesson here seems to be that the life of selfish pleasure ends in cynicism, and cynicism in moral death:—that of *Wages* (P. 74, x), that Morality which is without faith in the future life can have no secure foundation or trustworthy vital impulse. |
60	St. v *The crime of sense:* Only scorn and moral depravation survive in the worn-out sensualist: —"lust hard by hate," in Milton's phrase.
—	*The Two Voices:*—the conflict in a soul between Scepticism and Faith.
75	XI St. 3 *the scrawl:* Some sort of sea-crustacean. —The word is a modified, or rather an intensified derivative of *crawl*.
76	*The Voyage.* Life as Energy, in the great ethical sense of the word,—Life as the pursuit of the Ideal,—is figured in this brilliantly-descriptive allegory.

85 St. III *The crescent-bark:* Boat of the Moon towards the end of her first quarter.

89 *The Lotos-Eaters:*—placed by Herodotus on the Libyan coast, seemingly in Tripoli south of Malta. The fruit is described as "in sweetness resembling the date"; a wine was prepared from it.—The foundation-story of this poem is given in the *Odyssey*, IX, 82-115:—but the Olympus of the same (VI, 42-46), and the Lucretian repetition (III, 18-22), with other reminiscences from ancient song, must have entered into the varied landscape here set before us.

— St. 2 *Slow-dropping veils:* This image was suggested by the lofty waterfall of the Cirque of Gavarnie, in the French Pyrenees. St. 3 *galingale:* generally used of *Cyperus longus*, one of the Sedges: but the Papyrus species is here intended.—P. 93, St. VII *moly:* "so the gods call it," according to Homer (Od. X, 305): the magical medicinal plant

That Hermes once to wise Ulysses gave

to protect him against the spells of Circe.

94 *The Voyage of Maeldune:* The original story will be found in Joyce's *Celtic Legends*. Most of the details, however, are here due to the Poet's invention.

102 XVII St. III *coronach:* death-wail.

103 XVIII This, with XXXVI and XXXVII, is one of the songs inserted between the different cantos of the *Princess*.—The "*horns of Elfland*" were suggested by the bugle-echoes over the Lake of Killarney.

— XIX This lovely song, one of the triumphs of English double-rhyming, is extracted from the *Brook* Idyll, and inevitably suffers a little when not broken into sections by intervening blank-verse.

103 St. 3 *thorps:* villages.—P. 104, St. 2 *willow-weed:* commonly known as Great Willow-herb; *Epilobium hirsutum* of Linnaeus.

105 *The Daisy:*—Records Tennyson's journey with his wife in 1851; beginning with the Western Riviera.

— St. 2 *Turbìa:* a village beyond Nice; said to be so named from the *Trophaea Augusti*, a monument of which some fragments remain, built to commemorate the victories of that Emperor over the natives. St. 4 *campanili:* the tall Church bell-towers common in Italy. St. 6 *Cogoletto:* between Savona and Genoa; the traditional birthplace of Columbus.—P. 106, St. 4 *that hall:* In the Palazzo Ducale. It contains clever plaster statues of celebrated Genoese citizens. St. 5 *Cascinè:* the Hyde Park of Florence: *Boboli:* Gardens of the Pitti Palace, long the Grand-ducal residence.

107 St. 4 *The rich Virgilian rustic measure:* the passage referred to is from the second Georgic; —hence the epithet *rustic*. Vergil is here celebrating the beauty of Italy,—indeed, of his own part of Italy,—which he felt at once with all the sense of Roman dignity, and with all the sentiment in regard to landscape which modern life has so largely developed. This union of the old world and the new, managed with that perfect art in which he is First Master absolute, gives to Vergil's landscape a force and glow and tenderness which render his lines a haunting memory and melody to all who have once felt their magic.—Shall I tell, he says here, of the sea on each side Italy,

> Anne lacus tantos? te, Lari maxume, teque
> Fluctibus et fremitu adsurgens Benace marino?

In this and the following piece the poet has made some attempt to imitate,—not the exact metre,—but the effect of the Horatian Alcaic. Readers with an ear will notice the slightly

107 different character given to the fourth line in No. XXI by the accentual dactyl.

— St. 5 *The Lariano:* name of the steamer upon the Lake of Como, formerly *Larius*. *That fair port:* possibly, Varenna, above which is visible a ruin named Torre del Vezio.

— St. 6 *Agavè:* the Yucca.

108 XXI The life of Mr. Maurice, edited by his son, (1884), Vol. II, p. 212, says: "The post, one morning, brought a letter containing the Poet Laureate's lines of sympathy, and the invitation to visit his young godson, which Whewell declared to be the most perfect specimen of its kind in the language." Maurice thus notices the request in a letter of 29 Sep. 1852:

"Alfred Tennyson has done me the high honour of asking me to be godfather to his child . . . I accept the office with thankfulness and fear. It was to please his wife."

The scenery here described is that around the Poet's house Farringford, by Freshwater.

— St. 2 *Who give the Fiend himself his due:* Mr. Maurice's dismissal from his post in King's College, (alluded to in l. 3, 4), was the result of the interpretation placed by him upon a word darkly and imperfectly expressing one of those ideas which the human mind is equally unable to escape from or to define: and the line quoted must be taken as only a playful poetical rendering of his opinions—as it were, "give the worst of men their due."—Compare *In Memoriam*, No. LIV.

The following extract, which I am allowed to quote from a letter written (June 23, 1830) to Mr. Gladstone, by Mr. Arthur Hallam, shows the deep impression produced upon him by the good and gifted man to whom this Poem was addressed.

"I have to-day seen Rogers [now Lord

PAGE
108 Blachford], who tells me . . . that you know Maurice. I know nothing better suited to a letter of somewhat a serious kind than an exhortation to cultivate an acquaintance, which, from all I have heard, must be invaluable. I do not myself know Maurice, but I know well many whom he has known, and whom he has moulded, like a second Nature, and these, too, men eminent for intellectual power, to whom the presence of a commanding spirit would in all other cases be a signal rath[er] for rivalry than reverential acknowledgement. [The] effect which he has produced on the minds of many at Cambridge by the single creation of that society, the Apostles, (for the spirit though not the form *was* created by him) is far greater than I can dare to calculate, and will be felt both directly and indirectly in the age that is before us. By the bye, I hope you will buy and read Alfred Tennyson's poems. Any bookseller will get them for you: they are published by Effingham Wilson. I am sure you will perceive their extraordinary merit."

110 *Northern Farmer, Old Style:*—Additional Glossary. St. I 'asta beän *hast thou been:* thoort *thou art:* moänt 'a *may not have.* St. II point *pint.* St. III 'issén *himself:* towd *told:* boy *by.* St. IV Larn'd a ma' beä *learned he may be;*—a stands for *he* in this dialect:—a cast oop *he cast up against me.*—P. 111, St. V owt *ought.* St. VI 'Siver *Howsoever:* boy 'um *by him.* St. VII stubb'd *broken up for cultivation.* St. VIII moind *remember:* boggle *bogle,* haunting spirit: the lot *piece of waste:* raäved an' rembled *tore up and threw away.*—P. 112, St. IX Keäper's it wur *It was the gamekeeper's ghost:* toäner *the one or the other:* at 'soize *at the assizes.* St. X Dubbut *Do but:* yows *ewes.* St. XI ta-year *this year:* thruff *through:* haäte oonderd *eight hundred.* St. XII thutty *thirty.*—P. 113, St. XIII a moost *he must:* cauve *calve:*

PAGE	
110	hoälms *holms,* mounds of slightly rising ground (*Skeat*). St. XIV quoloty *quality,* the gentry: thessén *themselves:* sewerloy *surely.* St. XV howd *hold:* Sartin-sewer *Certain sure.* St. XVI Huzzin' an' maäzin' *Worrying with a hiss and astonishing:* kittle *boiler.* St. XVII atta *art thou:* 'toättler *teetotaller:* a's hallus i' the owd taäle *is always telling the same old story:* floy *fly.*
114	*Northern Farmer, New Style.*—St. I 'erse *horse.* St. II craw to pluck *matter to dispute:* woä then *go slower, lad.* St. III lass *daughter.*— P. 115, St. VI as 'ant nowt *as has nothing.* St. VII weänt 'a *will not have:* ligs *lies.* St. VIII shut on *clear of:*—P. 116 i' the grip *in the little draining-ditch.* St. X burn *born.* St. XI esh *ash.*—P. 117, St. XIII ammost *almost:* 'id *hidden away:* tued an' moil'd *put himself in a stew and toiled.* St. XIV run oop *his land ran up:* brig *bridge.*
118	*The Northern Cobbler.*—St. I. disolut *desolate:* sa 'ot *so hot:* 'eät *heat.* St. II maäin-glad *very glad.* St. III fettle *put into order.*—P. 119, St. IV squad *slush:* fowt *fought.* St. V weär'd *bartered.* —P. 120, St. VI fo'mma *for me:* athurt *athwart.* —P. 121, St. IX in a tew *state of confusion:* ov 'ersen *of herself.* St. XI num-cumpus *non-compos,* fool.—P. 122, St. XIII oän sen *own self.* —P. 123, St. XV tha mun *thou must:* spanks 'is 'and *slaps it.* St. XVII meller *mellow.*— P. 124, St. XVIII wi'mma *with me.* St. XIX feät, *deft, handy:* thebbe *they be.*
124	XXV This and the two pieces following have been placed together as illustrating, in different modes, a Poet's thoughts about his own art.— *The Cock:* an old-fashioned Inn, just East of Temple Bar.—P. 126, St. 2 *raffs:* scamps.— P. 128, St. I *praising God:* image suggested of old by the attitude of a bird as he drinks.— P. 130, St. I *days that deal in ana:* a name given in France to books containing "the

PAGE

124   reported conversation, the table-talk of the learned"; *e.g.* Scaligerana :—(Hallam, *Literature of Europe*). St. 4 *boxes:* pew-like seats in the old taverns.

133   XXVIII One of a very few "experiments," (so the author has named them), in accordance as strictly with the Roman metrical rules founded upon Quantity, in opposition to Accent, as our language will admit. Great would probably be the gain, if English verse could not only be relieved of the commonplace element which rhyme, more or less, all but inevitably carries with it, but become also capable of reproducing the exquisite endless variety, the inner structural life, if I may so express it, of the ancient metres. But it is too late a day :—our language, in all probability, is too long formed and set, our poetical literature too rich and too intimately part of our national life, to permit this change, except by way of experiment.

134   XXIX, XXX, XXXI These lovely lyrics are prelusive to the great work of Tennyson's later years ;—the "first love" to which, perhaps more fortunate than Milton, he has remained faithful. An Italian romance upon the *Donna di Scalotta*,—in which Camelot, unlike the Celtic tradition, was placed near the sea,—suggested No. XXIX. It is under the very different guise of the maid of Astolat that the legend reappears in the *Idylls of the King*.—P. 136, St. 2 *Galaxy:* the Milky Way.

141   XXXI St. 2 *the holy Grail:* the Chalice of the Last Supper.

142   XXXII A far-off and idealized reminiscence of the old legend proper to the Eve of Saint Agnes, it should be observed, seems to inspire the Nun in whose mouth this hymn is placed. St. 2 *argent round:* Moon at the full.—P. 143, St. 2 *One* (l. 10) was originally printed *Are* by error. Among all Tennyson's many metrical suc-

S

PAGE
142   cesses, these lines appear to me eminently felicitous.

144   XXXV This is the song of Queen Mary in the play so named, after she has learned that England and Philip hate her.

145   XXXVIII The Mother's song in the *Sea Dreams.*

146   XXXIX–XLV It is a matter of regret to me that the scheme of this little book did not allow *Maud,*—of all the Author's poems perhaps the most powerful, the most intensely lyrical,—to be integrally included. The whole possesses such unity that some loss must be felt when portions are extracted. I hence offer this garland with much diffidence, and submit the same apology in case of the closing selection from *In Memoriam.*

—   XL St. I An echo of the rooks' cry may be heard in the third line: as the call-notes of lesser birds are audible in the *here, here, here* of St. III, P. 147.—St. VI *left the daisies rosy:* the crimson underside of the corolla, shown as the flower is lightly trodden on.

152   XLIV St. IV *mattock-harden'd hand:* of the field-labourer. The argument is: I am now lifted above that despair during which I grieved that my lot had not been that of the cottager, uneducated in the knowledge of that tremendous vision which the science of Stellar Astronomy discloses. It is the sentiment of the terrible lines of Lucretius:

> Nam cum suspicimus magni caelestia mundi
> Templa, super stellisque micantibus aethera fixum,
> Et venit in mentem solis lunaeque viarum,
> Tunc aliis oppressa malis in pectora cura
> Illa quoque expergefactum caput erigere infit,
> Nequae forte deum nobis inmensa potestas
> Sit, vario motu quae candida sidera verset.

153   St. VII *The dusky strand:* Image from the coloured line sometimes woven into ropes.

PAGE	
157	*Tears, idle tears.* — It may be doubted much whether the Greeks, our Masters in the boundaries and definitions, as in the laws of Art, would have consented to define any song written in their blank-verse form as a lyric, even if so deeply lyrical as this in diction and sentiment. The lines may, however, perhaps be held *super legem* in virtue of their beauty.
	These considerations, in some degree, apply also to the following pieces, XLVII–L, interspersed as songs in the four earliest *Idylls of the King*.
161	l.11 This poem, I have heard, was thought of by the Author whilst travelling between Narbonne and Perpignan;—hence, more or less, the local colour of the landscape.
165	*The Lord of Burleigh.* "At the present moment," said the *Times* of 22 August, 1884, "it may possibly interest some of our readers to be reminded that the new Duke of Wellington is the great-grandson of the rustic beauty who, as every reader of Tennyson is aware, being born a 'village maiden' of Shropshire, was suddenly elevated to the painful dignity of a peerage by her marriage with 'the Lord of Burleigh,' whom she and her parents had taken to be only a 'landscape painter.' From being plain 'Sarah Hoggins, of Bolas Magna in the county of Shropshire,' she found herself Countess of Exeter, and 'the burden of an honour unto which she was not born' threw her into a consumption, and caused her early death, only six years after her marriage. According to Burke and Lodge, her death took place in 1797; and the 'three fair children' of whom she became the mother were Brownlow, afterwards eleventh Earl and second Marquis of Exeter, Lord Thomas Cecil, and Lady Sophia Cecil. The last-named child, on reaching womanhood, married the Right Hon. Henry Manvers Pierrepont, of Conholt-Park,

PAGE	
165	Hants, brother of the second Earl Manvers. Their only child, a daughter, Augusta Sophia Anne, became in 1844 Lady Charles Wellesley; and her eldest son, Henry, has become within the last few days, by his uncle's death, the third Duke of Wellington."
168	*Lady Clara Vere de Vere.* This poem has so much personal animation, that the reader should bear in mind that it is intended only as a dramatic picture of imaginary characters.
170	LVI Founded on the suggestion of *Romeo and Juliet*, A. II, S. i : Young Adam Cupid ;—he that shot so trim When king Cophetua loved the beggar-maid.
171	LVII St. 9 *spence:* the Buttery.—P. 172, St. 1 *man-minded offset:* Queen Elizabeth. St. 2 A tremendous storm marked the night of Oliver Cromwell's death, and the tradition was that the Stork, as a Republican bird, at once quitted England. The Oak is here naturally imagined as a staunch old Tory :—hence he speaks of the Protector as the *gloomy brewer.* St. 4 *tea-cup times:* The genius of Pope has inseparably united the ideas of Tea and of the days of Queen Anne.—P. 178, St. 3 *the northern morning:* Aurora Borealis. St. 7 *that Thessalian growth:* the Oak of Dodona, long famous as a Hellenic oracle.
179	LVIII The Milkmaid's song from *Queen Mary;* —supposed to be overheard by Princess Elizabeth whilst living at Woodstock.
187	LXI Addressed to James Spedding, distinguished as an Editor of Lord Bacon's Works; a College friend of the Author.
190	LXII, LXIII, LXIV The high and statesmanlike tone, the wise moderation and farsight of these poems,—worthy of the great Henry Hallam,— may be well illustrated by an extract from a letter of his son Arthur to Mr. Gladstone (Jan. 1827, 67 Wimpole St.) :—

PAGE	
190	"If by a moderate man you mean one who sets a guard on his mind, lest it should become the lurking-place of faction ; . . . one who in all political contests never forgets the great interests of justice, and peace, and humanity amid the exclusive views of party ; such a man is indeed one of God's noblest creatures: may such moderation be yours and mine." That a schoolboy who had not yet reached his sixteenth birthday, and could think thus and write thus, should have owned a commanding influence over his most gifted contemporaries, was inevitable:—and the more so, because Arthur Hallam's letters show that he was not more conspicuous for singular youthful promise than for a deep and childlike humility of nature. Early as he was lost, enough remains to prove emphatically that the literal truth is in no way exceeded by the pictures of the past and the anticipations of the future set forth by his friend in his great memorial poem.
191	LXIII St. 3 *the triple forks:* Suggested by the old Latin phrase *trisulca fulmina*, descriptive of the thunderbolts of Jupiter.
194	*The Revenge.* This sea-fight (1591) was described at the time in his most powerful style by Grenville's kinsman, Sir Walter Ralegh, who thus made his first appearance as an author. As the tract, though included among Mr. Arber's excellent reprints, is little known, I quote the last words ascribed to the Vice-Admiral:—"Here die I, Richard Grenville, with a joyful and quiet mind, for that I have ended my life, as a true soldier ought to do, fighting for his country, queen, religion, and honour."
202	LXVI St. VI *Mighty Seaman:* Wellington lies by Nelson in the crypt of St. Paul's. *Assaye:* "General Wellesley's" first victory; fought 1803. P. 203 *that loud sabbath:* Waterloo.
207	LXVII Balaclava,—25 Oct. 1854. The charge

PAGE

207 lasted twenty-five minutes, and left more than two-thirds of our men slain or wounded.

209 LXVIII Sir Henry Lawrence took charge of Lucknow as Resident in March, 1857. The spread of rebellion in June confined him to the defence of the city, where he died of wounds on July 4. Brigadier Inglis, in succession, then defended Lucknow for twelve weeks, till it was relieved on September 25 by General Havelock, to whom Sir James Outram, (who accompanied as a volunteer), had generously ceded the exploit.

215 LXX *Cauteretz* is a lovely valley in the French Pyrenees; the visit here commemorated was in 1830.

— *In Memoriam.* Upon the difficulty of framing this selection I have already said a few words: (Note on p. 146). In no part of my task, I fear, are readers more likely to complain of omissions which the length prescribed for the volume has rendered inevitable. To aim at choosing on grounds of comparative excellence would have been unsatisfactory where excellence is so uniformly maintained, and a choice so made must have had a fragmentary character. My wish, in the main, has therefore been to select first the songs most directly setting forth the personal love and sorrow which inspired this great lyrical elegy, and then those, or some of those, in which the same motive-theme is developed in figures, or connected with the aspects of nature and of religious thought.

Arthur Henry, son to Henry and Julia Maria Hallam (by birth Elton of Clevedon Court), was born Feb. 1, 1811; educated at Eton and Cambridge; died suddenly Sep. 15, 1833 at Vienna; borne to England by sea, and buried 3 Jan. 1834 in Clevedon Church above the Severn.

216 LXXI St. 7 *How much of act:* the Freewill which

PAGE
216   sustains and animates life demands action from us imperatively.
219   LXXII St. 4 *Where the kneeling hamlet:* before the altar of some village church. St. 5 *tangle:* seaweed.
222   LXXVII St. 2 The Wye joins the Severn about twenty miles north of Clevedon.
225   LXXXIII This poem was specially admired by Arthur Hallam's younger brother Henry. He, too, lies at Clevedon, with a sister, also cut off in youth:—My readers, I think, will not hold it superfluous if I add the epitaph in which the depth of nature, the faith and tenderness of his aged Father, found expression ;—

His saltem accumulem donis, et fungar inani Munere.

"To the memory of Henry Fitzmaurice "Hallam : Born Aug. 31, 1824 : died at Siena "Oct. 25, 1850.
"In whose clear and vivid understanding, "sweetness of disposition and purity of life, an "image of his elder brother was before the eyes "of those who had most loved him. Distinguished "like him by early reputation and by the attach- "ment of many friends, he was, like him, also "cut off by a short illness in a foreign land.
"His father, deeply sensible of the blessing in "having possessed such children as are com- "memorated in these tablets, submits to the "righteous Will of Heaven which has ordained "him to be their survivor."

—   St. 1 *the barren bush:* leafless: *the sea-blue bird of March:* the kingfisher, noticed by the author in North East Lincolnshire as then coming up inland. The sea which adorns the coast of our southern counties, Cornwall especially, emerald interchanged with ultramarine, answers to the epithet here given.

—   LXXXIV St. 1 *maze of quick:* every tangled thorn buds forth.

PAGE
226   LXXXV St. 1 *the crescent prime:* takes the hue of advancing Spring.

—   LXXXVI St. 1 *Doors:* of No. 67, Wimpole Street.

227   LXXXVII Refers to the shiftings of land and sea in geological time.

230   XCI St. 2 *the field of time:* as having no future life. St. 3 *want-begotten rest:* the passive content of ignorance and inexperience.

232   XCV St. 2 *thy sister: i.e.* Woman, in virtue of her devouter nature, and, consequently, firmer faith. St. 3 *the flesh and blood:* Christ as Son of God. St. 4 *such a type:* The vague mode of scepticism here indicated often recognizes Our Lord as a model for life. "Such a faith" is, hence, the sense required by the Poet's argument.

—   XCVI St. 2 *in closest words:* in a strictly dogmatic argument : *a tale:* the Gospels.—P. 233, St. 2 *those wild eyes:* Natives of the Pacific islands.

234   XCVIII St. 2 *Time . . . Life:* Figures for the mad agony of desperation.

238   CIV St. 1 *horned flood:* winding :—horns are borne commonly by the old river-personifications. St. 3 *orient star:* any rising star is here intended.

239   CVII St. 1 *Day:* the Fifteenth of September.— P. 240, St. 2 *coming care:* winter.

243   CXI St. 4 *the Christ that is to be:* The Second Advent.

An extract from a letter which unites the names and the poetry of Arthur Hallam and Alfred Tennyson will be the fittest ending to these imperfect notes.

A. H. Hallam, *The Lodge, Malvern,* 14 Sep. 1829; *to W. E. Gladstone, at Mr. Gaskell's, Thornes House, Wakefield.*

"I am glad you liked my queer piece of

work about Timbuctoo [subject of the Cambridge English Verse Prize for 1829]. I wrote it in a sovereign vein of poetic scorn for anybody's opinion, who did not value Plato, and Milton, just as much as I did. The natural consequence was that ten people out of twelve laughed, or opened large eyes; and the other two set about praising highly, what was plainly addressed to them, not to people in general. So my vanity would fain persuade me, that, like some of my betters, I "fit audience found, tho' few." My friend Tennyson's poem, which got the prize, will be thought by the ten sober persons afore mentioned twice as absurd as mine: and to say the truth by striking out his prose argument the Examiners have done all in their power to verify the concluding words "All was night." The splendid imaginative power that pervades it will be seen through all hindrances. I consider Tennyson as promising fair to be the greatest poet of our generation, perhaps of our century."

INDEX OF FIRST LINES

	PAGE
Again at Christmas did we weave	241
All along the valley, stream that flashest white	215
And Willy, my eldest-born, is gone, you say, little Anne	42
Ask me no more: the moon may draw the sea	144
As sometimes in a dead man's face	224
A still small voice spake unto me	60
At Flores in the Azores Sir Richard Grenville lay	194
Banner of England, not for a season, O banner of Britain, hast thou	209
Be near me when my light is low	234
Birds in the high Hall-garden	146
Break, break, break	214
Bury the Great Duke	200
Calm is the morn without a sound	219
Come into the garden, Maud	149
Come not, when I am dead	144
Come, when no graver cares employ	108
Comrades, leave me here a little, while as yet 'tis early morn	20
Could we forget the widow'd hour	233
'Courage!' he said, and pointed toward the land	89
Deep on the convent-roof the snows	142
Doors, where my heart was used to beat	226
Dosn't thou 'ear my 'erse's legs, as they canters awaäy?	114
Dost thou look back on what hath been	236
Do we indeed desire the dead	234

	PAGE
Flow down, cold rivulet, to the sea	143
Glory of warrior, glory of orator, glory of song	74
Go not, happy day	147
Half a league, half a league	207
Hapless doom of woman happy in betrothing	144
He past ; a soul of nobler tone	235
Her arms across her breast she laid	170
Her eyes are homes of silent prayer	231
He rose at dawn and, fired with hope	75
He tasted love with half his mind	224
How pure at heart and sound in head	238
I built my soul a lordly pleasure-house	11
I climb the hill : from end to end	240
I come from haunts of coot and hern	103
I dream'd there would be Spring no more	237
I envy not in any moods	230
If one should bring me this report	221
I had a vision when the night was late	54
I have led her home, my love, my only friend	151
I hear the noise about thy keel	219
In her ear he whispers gaily	165
In Love, if Love be Love, if Love be ours	158
In those sad words I took farewell	223
I read, before my eyelids dropt their shade	3
I see the wealthy miller yet	179
Is it, then, regret for buried time	226
I was the chief of the race—he had stricken my father dead	94
Lady Clara Vere de Vere	168
Late, late, so late ! and dark the night and chill	157
Like souls that balance joy and pain	138
Love thou thy land, with love far-brought	191
My good blade carves the casques of men	140
My love has talk'd with rocks and trees	238
Now fades the last long streak of snow	225
Of old sat Freedom on the heights	190
Oh yet we trust that somehow good	235

	PAGE
O Lady Flora, let me speak	79
Old Yew, which graspest at the stones . .	227
O let the solid ground	146
O living will that shalt endure	243
O love, what hours were thine and mine . .	105
O mighty-mouth'd inventor of harmonies . .	133
Once more the gate behind me falls . . .	170
On either side the river lie	134
One writes, that 'Other friends remain' . .	228
O plump head-waiter at The Cock . . .	124
O that 'twere possible	154
O thou that after toil and storm	232
Our doctor had call'd in another, I never had seen him before	38
Peace ; come away : the song of woe . . .	223
Revered, beloved—O you that hold . . .	1
Ring out, wild bells, to the wild sky . . .	242
Risest thou thus, dim dawn, again . . .	239
Rivulet crossing my ground	148
Shame upon you, Robin	179
Slow sail'd the weary mariners and saw . .	88
Still on the tower stood the vane . . .	186
Sweet after showers, ambrosial air . . .	237
Sweet and low, sweet and low	145
Sweet is true love tho' given in vain, in vain .	159
Tears, idle tears, I know not what they mean .	157
Tears of the widower, when he sees . . .	220
The Danube to the Severn gave	222
The lesser griefs that may be said . . .	229
The plain was grassy, wild and bare . . .	101
The rain had fallen, the Poet arose . . .	131
There rolls the deep where grew the tree . .	227
The splendour falls on castle walls . . .	103
The time draws near the birth of Christ . .	230
The wind, that beats the mountain, blows . .	187
This truth came borne with bier and pall . .	215
Tho' truths in manhood darkly join . . .	232
'Tis well ; 'tis something ; we may stand . .	221
Turn, Fortune, turn thy wheel and lower the proud	158

	PAGE
Unwatch'd, the garden bough shall sway	241
Waäit till our Sally cooms in, fur thou mun a' sights to tell	118
Wailing, wailing, wailing, the wind over land and sea	48
We left behind the painted buoy	76
We were two daughters of one race	164
What does little birdie say	145
Wheer 'asta beän saw long and meä liggin' 'ere aloän?	110
When Lazarus left his charnel-cave	231
When rosy plumelets tuft the larch	225
With blackest moss the flower-plots	159
With one black shadow at its feet	161
With weary steps I loiter on	222
You ask me, why, tho' ill at ease	190
You might have won the Poet's name	132
You must wake and call me early, call me early, mother dear	31

Printed by R. & R. CLARK, *Edinburgh.*

www.ingramcontent.com/pod-product-compliance
Lightning Source LLC
Chambersburg PA
CBHW032123230426
43672CB00009B/1835